Touching the Hem of His Garment

Seeking God's Presence Through Prayer

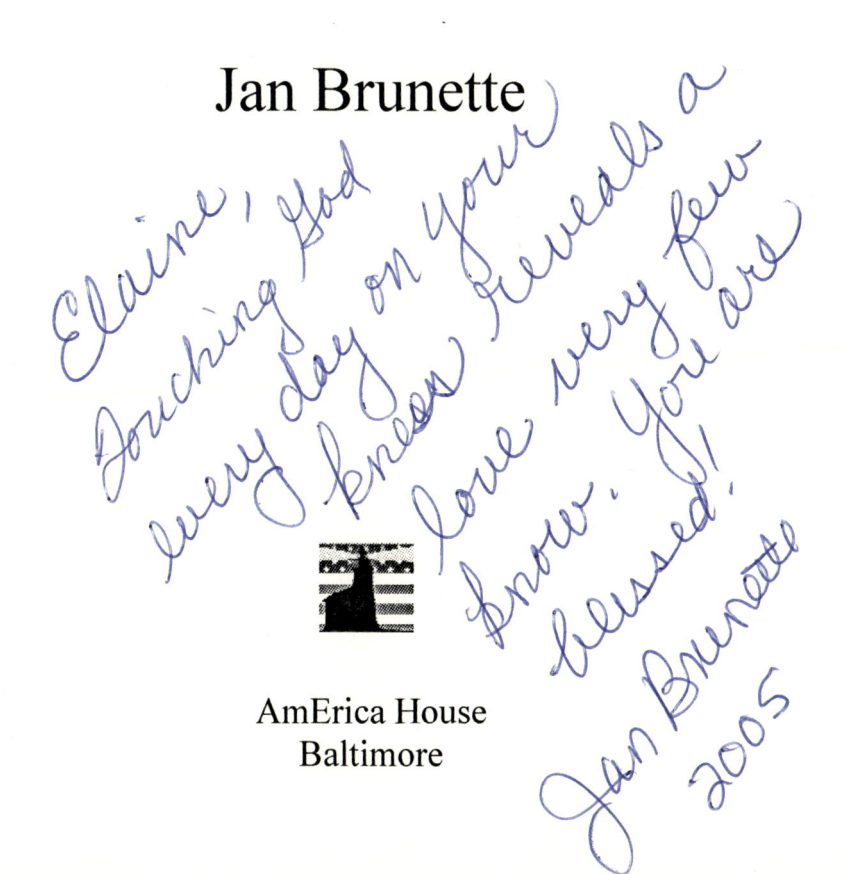

Jan Brunette

AmErica House
Baltimore

© 2001 by Jan Brunette.

All rights reserved. No part of this book may be reproduced in any form without written permission from the publishers, except by a reviewer who may quote brief passages in a review to be printed in a newspaper or magazine.

First printing

ISBN: 1-59129-025-2
PUBLISHED BY AMERICA HOUSE BOOK PUBLISHERS
www.publishamerica.com
Baltimore

Printed in the United States of America

Unless otherwise indicated, all Scripture quotations are from the Holy Bible, New International Version, copyright 1973, 1978, 1984 International Bible Society. Used by permission of Zondervan Bible Publishers.

Scripture references marked RSV are from the Revised Standard Version of the Bible, © 1946, 1952, 1971, 1973, Division of Christian Education, National Council of the Churches in the USA.

Scripture references marked Amplified Bible are from THE AMPLIFIED BIBLE, Old Testament copyright © 1965, 1987 by the Zondervan Corporation. The Amplified New Testament copyright © 1958, 1987 by the Lockman Foundation. Used by permission.

Scripture references marked TLB are taken from the The Living Bible, copyright 1971 by Tyndale House Publishers, Wheaton, Ill. Used by permission.

In loving memory of my parents, Martin and Clara Yungmann, who revealed God's goodness to me through example and instruction.

In loving memory of my brother, Marty Yungmann, Jr. and my sister, Marlene Hubach, who dedicated their lives to serving the Lord and others.

Contents

Introduction		7
1.	A Divine Connection – Approaching the Father	9
2.	A Torn Curtain – Praying in Jesus' Name	15
3.	The Garden's Agony – Desiring the Father's will	23
4.	The Heavenly Hook-up – The Interceding of the Holy Spirit	31
5.	A Brave Woman – Finding Healing in His Touch	39
6.	An Untouchable Outcast – "Am I Worthy?"	47
7.	The Pleading Father – Overcoming Unbelief Through Prayer	55
8.	A Persistent Widow – Never Give Up!	63
9.	The Caring Centurion – Praying for Others	71
10.	A Heaven-bound Thief – Claiming Promises	83

11.	A Grateful Leper – Having a Thankful Heart	97
12.	The Praise of a King – God Deserves Praise	109
13.	A High Priestly Example – Bringing Glory to the Father	119
14.	At His Feet – Listen and Grow in the Word	129

INTRODUCTION

Stoutly standing before the throne of grace, the young man desired to understand why prayers he offered never appeared to be answered. Looking at God, he said, "You disappoint me, God. I prayed for so many things and you rejected most of them. Where did I go wrong? Or are you a God who enjoys seeing your loved ones suffer?"

Silently the Father peered into the young man's eyes. Without saying a word, He reached out His hand and led him to a room filled with millions of bottles, each with a person's name on it. Not understanding the reason for all the bottles, the young man turned to God and curiously asked, "What is stored in all these bottles?"

The Father responded, "When my loved ones cried in the midst of prayers, I stored their tears. When they ached for answers and wept because of lack of understanding, I stored their tears. As they grew in their love for me, and their tears changed to tears of love, I stored their tears. All were valued. All heard. All understood.

"When I looked upon you in love, I cried with you. I made some tough decisions. But these decisions were not intended to cause more pain but to draw you into the presence of My Son. That was my ultimate goal and eternal purpose."

As the young man looked again in the Father's eyes, he saw a compassion never known before. As the Father's tears rolled down His cheeks, the young man picked up a bottle and stored the love tears within. Now he understood. Prayer reveals love – love filled with compassion and goodness, all at the same time. The young man's prayers were answered. The Father created the likeness of His Son inside him, but he had failed to see it. Now his bottle of the Father's tears would serve to remind him of One whose only desire was his highest good.

The glory of the Father is revealed through prayer. It cannot be a magic potion, a selfish cry for help, or a method of imposing our will upon God. Drawing closer to the Father, the Son and the Holy Spirit, we grow in understanding and wisdom – His wisdom. Our desires change and the ultimate goal of prayer evolves into a power source led by the Spirit, through the Son, and for the glory of the Father. As you read this book, may you further comprehend with all the saints, the true, unconditional love of the Almighty God and desire a prayer life that reflects an amazing relationship.

Jan Brunette

1
A DIVINE CONNECTION
Approaching the Father

Huddled in my closet, exhausted, weeping, I stretched out my hands to the only one who could help. "Dear God, Your face do I seek." Sitting at the bottom of a pit, I looked up, the only place with any semblance of light.

Reminded of the verse in Psalm 18:6, I opened my Bible and read, *In my distress I called to the Lord: I cried to my God for help. From his temple he heard my voice; my cry came before Him, into his ears.*

"Dear Abba Father, you alone can help me to understand the purpose for this hole. Fear has engulfed me and its threat will not go away. I am closed in on all sides. My soul's only hope is in You. Please come down from Your heavenly dwelling place and pull me out of this pit."

Understanding that prayer touched God's heart, I sought its power. I claimed the comfort and strength of the Holy Spirit, the source of all prayer. I possessed no other avenue of relief.

I concluded that God in His goodness loved me. I cherished the thought but felt no release from the fear. Seeking God had to be the answer. I needed to comprehend this God that I believed in so strongly. Who was He anyway?

Someone once quoted the verse, *Call to me and I will answer you and tell you great and unsearchable things you do not know* (Jeremiah 33:3) and referred to it as God's telephone number. I opened my Amplified Bible for further explanation. *Call to me and I will answer you and show you great and mighty things, fenced in and hidden, which you do not know (do not distinguish and recognize, have knowledge of and understand.)* My hungering soul ached for refreshment. Claiming this verse, I began a word and Scripture study that continues to this day. It became my divine connection to a loving, protecting Father that surrounded me with His love especially during this agonizing episode of my life.

Call...and I will answer – promise deeply embedded in the heart and soul of God. A hammer struck over my head was not necessary. His quiet, gentle voice within my spirit touched me. His everlasting arms surrounded me and held me close, even though within myself pain and a lack of understanding existed. Trust moved in through His Holy Spirit as I looked heavenward and called, trusting an answer.

Tell you great and unsearchable things. The Hebrew context indicates fenced in, hidden, "walled up to the sky" revelations. God answers from His holy sanctuary, His heavenly throne room. What He plans to send transcends earthly happiness or wealth.

His goal is to create in His chosen children the likeness of Jesus Christ Himself – a servant heart, a loving spirit, a forgiving tongue. The results far surpassed anything my human mind could conjure up or expect. Into my very being entered a transcendent glory of a God not known before and a blessedness beyond all comprehension. As my heart, mind and soul called, His wonders never ceased. They were there for me then and for all eternity.

You do not know – cannot understand, recognize or distinguish. My mind wants to understand what's going on. It craves an explanation. But trust says, "Believe that what God is going to do is nothing short of incredible." As a child, I learned the verse in Proverbs 3:5,6 *Trust in the Lord with all your heart and lean not on your own understanding; in all your ways acknowledge him, and he will make your paths straight.*

My mind need not understand. My spirit need only rest in my Rock – my solid ground *To you I call, O Lord my Rock; do not turn a deaf ear to me. For if you remain silent, I will be like those who have gone down to the pit. Hear my cry for mercy as I call to you for help, as I lift my hands toward your Holy Place.* (Psalm 28:1,2)

Life was crumbling around me. My spouse of seventeen years died at the early age of thirty-seven, preceded by two, long, painful years of surgeries, hospital tests and treatments. His death heaped on me more uncertainty, as I was required to go back to work, move to a new location and raise four small children alone. The emotional load crushed my very being. Sleepless nights and fear surfaced. While my personal life rocked like mighty waves around me, I found the Source of solid footing. My loving Father came into view and hugged me. He became my Fortress, my unfailing strength. I discovered that my security did not rest in the world around me but in the God who had made His throne in my heart. His presence never left – it had been there all the time.

The distress of my momentary hardships passed slowly. But in the process, my eyes opened to new revelations – new love – new strength. The ability to go on rested not in myself but in the God who saved me.

The desire emerged to seek God first, to concentrate on the kingdom He had to offer, and to praise Him without ceasing even during pain and tribulation. Keeping my eyes focused on Jesus, the Author and Perfecter of my faith, fear began to dissipate. Peace filled my spirit instead. His divine connection proved true – *Call to me and I will answer you and tell you great and unsearchable things you do not know.*

1. DIGGING INTO HIS WORD

"For I know the plans I have for you," declares the Lord, "plans to prosper you and not to harm you, plans to give you hope and a future. Then you will call upon me and come and pray to me, and I will listen to you. You will seek me and find me when you seek me with all your heart. I will be found by you," declares the Lord. Jeremiah 29:11-14

While in Babylonian exile, the people of Israel were encouraged by Jeremiah with God's promises of guidance and hope. So in our times of "exile," His promises ring true for us as well. If we call and pray, listen and seek Him with all our heart, He will listen.

The following verses confirm that promise. As you read the verses, write on a sheet of paper what is required of us, and the promise of God.

Psalm 25:8-12; Psalm 32:6-8; Psalm 50:14,15; Isaiah 30:19; Isaiah 58:9a; Isaiah 56:6,7; James 4:8

As you read Ephesians 3:12,16-19 below, meditate on the rewards in Christ received through complete surrender in prayer.

In him and through faith in him we may approach God with freedom and confidence...I pray that out of his glorious riches he may strengthen you with power through his Spirit in your inner being, so that Christ may dwell in your hearts through faith. And I pray that you, being rooted and established in love, may have power, together with all the saints, to grasp how wide and long and high and deep is the love of Christ, and to know this love that surpasses knowledge – that you may be filled with all the fullness of God. Herein rests the purpose of God's divine connection!

Prayer: Abba Father, Your goodness is beyond comprehension. Open my eyes to the generosity of love that is endowed upon me – even, and especially, during difficult times. Thank You for Your steadfast love and faithfulness that surrounds me as I seek Your face in prayer. Amen.

2
A Torn Curtain
Praying in Jesus' Name

The sound of tearing flesh, the cry of agony and the spiritual anguish were unfathomable. As others watched this bloodied man encounter all kinds of torture, a wide gamut of emotions spilled out among the members of the crowd. What horrible crime had He committed that was so deserving of this insurmountable punishment?

Some men laughed and jeered, "He was so great at saving others, let's see if He can save himself." As they fought and gambled over His garments, greed and envy wrapped them tightly. They had no genuine concern for this man hanging on the center cross – this man who claimed to be a king. "Yeah, right – a king. Can you imagine a king whose reign would end this way? Come on. Come down from that cross if You're so mighty. Where are Your followers now, O King?"

From a near-by cross a voice could be heard. "Hey, O king, save all three of us. Why aren't You using Your mighty power to get us down from here?"

But another victim's heart feels compassion and encounters a transformation. He sees this torn, beaten man as touched in some way with a gentle, loving Spirit. He knows in his heart that this man is different. Mustering up every fiber of strength within him, he calls out to the other thief, "Leave Him alone. Don't you see who this is? He's not like us. He's not guilty of anything wrong. We deserve to be here. He doesn't."

Turning his head toward the man in the center, the second thief is awed at the tenderness in His eyes, even through all the hatred surrounding Him. He sees the compassion, the love, the forgiveness, the eternal Presence. "Please, O King, I know I'm not worthy. I know You're from another kingdom. When You arrive, please remember me. I want to be a part of Your life forever."

Almost choking from the burden of hanging on the cross for hours, the bloodied captive manages to muster up the strength to grant the second thief a blessing that will last him for eternity. "Today, young man, you will be with Me forever."

What calmness stirs in the heart of the young man! What joy overwhelms him in spite of the pain of that cross! He knows his life is not over, but just beginning. He knows the words of the King are true.

Tears stream down the faces of some women and a few followers of this man. It has happened all too quickly. Last night He was dragged away. Now He is bloodied and beaten, dying an excruciating, suffocating death. The former joy of His presence remains swallowed up in intense sorrow.

Sadly, the greatest anguish is not even visible. His very spirit is suffering the hellish, insurmountable sins of every person ever to exist on this earth.

He cries, "Father, You hate sin. I'm spilling my blood out for these people because I love them so much, but You can't look at me because of the sin. I feel empty. The void without You is incredibly deep. I've celebrated a oneness with You since eternity and now I only see Your rejection. That burden of sin is crushing Me. *My God, my God, why have you forsaken me?"* (Mark 15:34)

As His mother watches on, her inner being is pierced with sorrow. The torture of her soul, the weeping and the pain in her heart, is unbearable. As she looks on the face of her son, she knows that this is the purpose for which He was born. A reminder of Simeon's words eight days after the King's birth, rings true. *And a sword will pierce your own soul too.* (Luke 2:35)

While her thoughts are with Him, His thoughts turn to her. "Mother, I know you need to be taken care of. And I will not leave you alone."

"John, my beloved follower, I give My mother to you for safe-keeping. I rest her in your loving hands."

Bending His head in utter fatigue, the mighty King – the humble man – knows His work is finished. As He closes His eyes, He surrenders His spirit to the loving Father who had earlier rejected Him. The battle of hellish punishment is over.

The tearing of flesh is ended, only to be replaced by the tearing of the earth. As mountains rumble and shake, graves open and darkness covers the earth; a curtain in the Holy of Holies rips apart. That curtain, never opened before to anyone but the High Priest once a year, was now open to everyone. What could this mean?

And so, dear brothers, now we may walk right into the very Holy of Holies where God is, because of the blood of Jesus. This is the fresh, new life-giving way which Christ has opened up for us by tearing the curtain – his human body – to let us into the holy presence of God. And since this great High Priest of ours rules over God's household, let us go right in to God because we have been sprinkled with Christ's blood to make us clean, and because our bodies have been washed with pure water. Now we can look forward to the salvation God has promised us. There is no longer any room for doubt, and we can tell others that salvation is ours, for there is no question that he will do what he says. (Hebrews 10:19-23, The Living Bible)

The symbolism is evident in striking array. Jesus Christ, that bloodied man on the center cross, used His very flesh to open the wonders of heaven to us. Because full atonement for our sins was made, communication with His Father would no longer be blocked. The price of our access to freedom, our open-door policy to the Father, was the tearing of the curtain, His flesh.

Praying in Jesus' Name

What possible correlation is there between the torn curtain and the words " in Jesus' name" as used in prayer?

Before Jesus' death, no man could see the face of God and live. No one could approach the Father unless He was specifically called. God was hidden to man with no access to Him except through the High Priest. The line of communication with God the Father was not allowed as part of a person's daily life. A heavy wall of sin – a curtain – shielded the presence of the Almighty God.

When Jesus died on the cross, paying the heavy penalty for our load of sins, the curtain of His flesh and the curtain in the temple were ripped apart. The wall that obstructed our view of the presence of God was destroyed. The price for our penalty of sin was paid once and for all. Jesus, the High Priest, forever canceled any debts we owed for a lifetime of sin. Open communication with God the Father became available to us. He is ours to learn about, to approach, to fall in love with.

Jesus revealed a new love relationship to us. He not only embodied a full example of love for His Father but revealed the Father to us. Because of this, His name opens the heavens as we approach the very throne of God with our praise, our thanks, our petitions, our cries of desperation.

Therefore, since we have a great high priest who has gone through the heavens, Jesus the Son of God, let us hold firmly to the faith we profess. For we do not have a high priest who is unable to sympathize with our weaknesses, but we have one who has been tempted in every way, just as we are – yet was without sin. Let us then approach the throne of grace with confidence, so that we may receive mercy and find grace to help us in our time of need.* (Hebrews 4:14-16)

Jesus not only invites us to the throne of His Father, but joins us in our prayers. He does not leave us without help. *Therefore he is able to save completely those who come to God through him, because he always lives to intercede for them.* (Hebrews 7:25)

An ecstatic rush generates me when I realize that my prayers are not only reaching heavenward, but that "in Jesus' name" and by His power and love, my prayers are actually being seated at the very throne of God. And I don't need to worry about my own personal inadequacies in prayer, for Christ covers it with His love.

So often I have encountered people who felt that they could not pray unless there was a presence of formality and special vocabulary. But Jesus just wants us to talk, to communicate on a loving, friendship level. He desires our fellowship. He wants our love, our trust, our willing heart. There is so much to be gained through our walk with Jesus and it is in His name that we can grow in that walk. The formality and vocabulary may be there but if the heart is not right with Him and His Father, it has little value to Him. In His own words, He says, *"And when you pray, do not keep on babbling like pagans, for they think they will be heard because of their many words. Do not be like them, for your Father knows what you need before you ask him."* (Matthew 6:7,8)

However in the same sermon, He motivates us to pray with these words, *"Ask and it will be given to you; seek and you will find; knock and the door will be opened to you. For everyone who asks receives; he who seeks find; and to him who knocks, the door will be opened. Which of you, if his son asks for bread, will give him a stone? or if he asks for a fish, will give him a snake? If you, then though you are evil, know how to give good gifts to your children, how much more will your Father in heaven give good gifts to those who ask him"* (Matthew 7:7-11)

Ask, Seek and Knock

The story is told of a man who arrived in heaven. Immensely enthralled with his tour of all the glories to behold, confusion existed concerning one particular building. This huge warehouse held many different types of unopened gifts. After several days of observing it, the suspense overwhelmed him. He asked God, "Father, please explain to me the significance of the warehouse with all the unopened gifts." To this God responded, "Those were all the gifts I had for my people for which they never asked."

Many times our ignorance of prayer and our fear of it, keeps us from asking, seeking and knocking. Jesus invites us to pray using His name as our source of reference. He desires so much for us, especially in the realm of His heavenly kingdom and we have only to ask Him. *"I tell you the truth, anyone who has faith in me will do what I have been doing. He will do even greater things than these, because I am going to the Father. And I will do whatever you ask in my name, so that the Son may bring glory to the Father. You may ask me for anything in my name and I will do it."* (John 14:12-14)

Our ultimate purpose of prayer should always be to bring glory to the Father through the Son. Our love for Him will motivate us to pray for those things that create in us a beautiful, precious spirit – one that seeks the best for others and for ourselves. When our focus is on Jesus and the cross, our prayers will change. They will become less selfish and more in line with His desires. But growth in prayer using Jesus' name takes time. That's why He is always there to intercede for us. He wants to help us in the growth process. Ask, seek and knock. You will discover a Savior who will be the answer to all things. Through Him and in Him you will be given the answer, find your source of love and have miracles open up before you. Never doubt His desire to give His very best. He has a whole warehouse full of gifts just waiting for you.

2. DIGGING INTO HIS WORD

Therefore God exalted him to the highest place and gave him the name that is above every name, that at the name of Jesus every knee should bow, in heaven and on earth and under the earth, and every tongue confess that Jesus Christ is Lord, to the glory of God the Father. (Philippians 2:9-11)

Jesus opened the windows of heaven through His torn flesh on the cross. In His name, the name of authority, we are granted the following:

1. Power in His name – Refer to: John 1:1-4,14; Philippians 2:9-11; Colossians 1:15-20

2. Freedom in His name – Refer to: Ephesians 3:8-12; Colossians 1:20-23; Hebrews 4:14-16

3. Empowerment through His name – Refer to: Galatians 2:20-21; Hebrews 12:1-3; Colossians 2:6-7,9-15

Jesus Christ fulfilled the mission to which His Father called Him. Now resting at the Father's right hand, Jesus intercedes for us, His saints, and fills us with His mission of love and hope. Because of Him we claim the promise that God will *fill (us) with all joy and peace as (we) trust in him, so that (we) may overflow with hope by the power of the Holy Spirit.* (Romans 15:13 – parenthesis indicates change in pronoun)

Prayer: Dearest Jesus, thank You for opening a pathway of love to the Father by Your ultimate sacrifice on the cross. Help me never forget Your Presence in my prayer life as I daily approach the throne of grace in Your name. Amen

3
THE GARDEN'S AGONY
Desiring the Father's Will

No one could possibly comprehend the next steps the Master was determined to take. A sense of resolute intensity rested in His soul. The hour for eternal justification lay all too close.

Approaching the garden, eight men remained at the entrance. Upon request, three close companions followed the Master. Not sure what was expected, they only noticed how heavily their eyes drooped. Sleep beckoned them even though the man requested prayers. The Master looked at them with pleading eyes and said, *"My soul is overwhelmed with sorrow to the point of death. Stay here and keep watch with me."* (Matthew 36:38) A battle already consumed him – a battle of the will. Crushed by heavy agony, He needed to know their prayers would offer guidance and protection from the upcoming struggle. He hoped their companionship and comfort would relieve some the immense load cutting at His soul. If ever He needed them, it was now.

Moving forward to a quiet, dark place, the Master stooped and hunched over from an unbearable weight. Intense sorrow and bitter torment lashed at His soul. Seemingly the horrors of hell bit at His heels. Falling with His face to the ground, He cried, "My Abba, My Father, if is possible, please take this cup, this wine of your wrath and fury, from Me. It is more than I can bear. The eternal load of man's sin overwhelms Me. But because I love You and them and came to do Your will, I will do what You desire."

Rising from His place of prayer, He returned to His three chosen disciples only to find them asleep. Looking at Peter, one of the chosen men, he asked *"Could you men not keep watch with me for one hour? Watch and pray so that you will not fall into temptation. The spirit is willing, but the body is weak."* (Matthew 26:40,41) Did he know something they did not comprehend at this point? Couldn't they see the anguish He endured and the dangers they were in?

A second time, the Master returned to His place of prayer and cried, *"My Father, if it is not possible for this cup to be taken away unless I drink it, may your will be done."* (Matthew 26:42)

Sorrow shrouded the man. Every fiber of His will desired an alternate plan. The lingering horror increased. Loneliness began to invade His heart and soul. He knew His Father would forsake Him – something He could not bear to imagine.

Returning again to His three sleeping friends, He, Jesus, realized they were too tired to help Him face His bitter struggle. Setting His face toward the soon-to-be future of denial, desertion, distrust, torment of soul, treachery, betrayal, mocking and death itself, He returned a third time to pray.

Sometime during His prayer and pleadings, an angel appeared. The angel's purpose and task was to submerge Jesus with strength and to comfort Him as best he could. But the anguish was not over. Jesus' prayer became more earnest. The pores of His body opened and blood flooded from them. Even the battle with the will entangled Him so fervently that His body reacted. Already He shed blood for those He loved. With one last plea, He cried, "Abba, Father, if there is any other way to glorify You and save man, please take this cup from Me. But if it cannot be taken away unless I drink it, may Your will be done."

The wrestling with God, completed in darkness and

agony, found itself replaced with peace, light and joy. His battle with the will was over. In submission and obedience, He walked toward the agonizing torture of body and soul to come.

Let us fix our eyes on Jesus, the author and perfecter of our faith, who for the joy set before him endured the cross, scorning its shame, and sat down at the right hand of the throne of God. Consider him who endured such opposition from sinful men, so that you will not grow weary and lose heart. Hebrews 12:2,3

Prayer – a Struggle to Do the Father's Will

No one stood behind the candy counter as I eyed the choices of colors, types and flavors. With penny in hand, my mouth watered. "Where is the lady? I'm ready to buy my candy." I waited all day, knowing I would walk downtown after school to buy that one piece of candy. Pink jawbreakers, bubble gum, licorice, taffy all beckoned me.

"Take one, Janet. No one is looking," a voice said inside. I scanned the front of the store. "You're right. Everyone is at the back of the store," I thought. In my seven-year-old mind, I struggled between wanting the candy and knowing it was wrong to take it. Glancing back and forth several times, a part of me cried, "Please, oh please, come soon. I know it's wrong to take this candy. I don't want to do it." The taunting voice kept pushing me to take it, but my hand just wouldn't move. I knew it was wrong. Being side-tracked by my thoughts, I didn't notice the clerk approaching. Like music to my ears, she spoke, "What can I get you?" Startled but relieved, I chose my favorite taffy and burst out of the store. "I did it! I did the right thing," I cried.

As a seven-year-old, I proved too young to understand temptation and the struggle with the will. But the brief encounter with Satan's lies remains deeply embedded in my mind still today. I rest in the assurance that His Spirit fed my spirit with the truth. My struggle to do the Father's will proved evident and I praise Him for the strength to resist.

The phrase "if it be thy will" left a stigma with me in my younger years that remained unresolved until my forties. Feelings of doubt in His goodness often entered my mind. "Why pray, if you're just going to say, '**if** it be thy will'. He probably won't give it to me anyway." Much research, Bible study and a time of brokenness entered my life before full comprehension evolved.

Desiring to do the Father's will remains a dominant part of my life today. Through Scripture and prayers, through His wisdom and guidance, through tears and anguish, His will now absorbs much of my thinking. My heart aches to fulfill what He has called me to do. Although I fall short, He continues to assure me of His grace and lovingly says, "I understand."

Learning from Jesus

"My food is to do the will of Him who sent me and to finish His work." (John 4:34) Jesus never lost sight of His purpose – to do His Father's will. He knew what God desired of Him and He boldly announced it. His unwavering desire to reflect the Father's love moved Him step by step through His lonely but fulfilling trek in life.

Many people today believe that they are living at the point of their utmost limit of tolerance. I have often heard others say, "I can't take it any more!" Yet days, months and years down the road, they are still moving ahead. Many are only surviving but some have grown into a unique and special relationship with a God who loves, gives and sacrifices all for them. They understand how wonderful and beneficial it is to desire and try to fulfill the Father's will in their lives. Because of Christ's example in the garden – a garden remembered for its agony – renewed strength becomes a part of their lives.

Out of love for His Father, Jesus followed His every command. The words spoken, the deeds done, the direction of each day, fulfilled His Father's will. *"For I did not speak of my own accord, but the Father who sent me commanded me what to say and how to say it. I know that his command leads to eternal life. So whatever I say is just what the Father has told me to say."* (John 12:49,50) *"But the world must learn that I love the Father and that I do exactly what my Father has commanded me."* (John 14:31).

As we focus on Jesus and the kingdom He called us into, our thoughts and minds begin to center on that same goal – to do the will of the Father. God, the Father, sent us here upon this earth for one purpose, namely, to do those things He called us to do. *For we are God's workmanship, created in Christ Jesus to do good works, which God prepared in advance for us to do.* (Eph. 2:8,9) Not only are we created to be special, but that creation rested in Jesus Christ Himself. We are not an accident. He called us from His heavenly kingdom to do His work, His will. Good works proceed from those who develop a loving relationship with God, the Father. But God's assurance doesn't end there. He also promises that our good works are already planned and prepared for us. He knows what He wants us to do. We have only to ask for wisdom and direction and believe that He will provide it.

No task will be beyond His ability to help. Will it sometimes take us out of our comfort zone? Most definitely! Christ Jesus Himself serves as a genuine example of that. But God's will done God's way never lacks God's supply. God promises in Scripture, *May the God of peace, who through the blood of the eternal covenant brought back from the dead our Lord Jesus, that great Shepherd of the sheep, equip you with everything good for doing his will, and may he work in us what is pleasing to him, through Jesus Christ, to whom be glory for ever and ever. Amen.* (Hebrews 13:20,21)

If the ground is prepared, the deeds provided for and strength promised, what is left? Obedience! Now it remains in our body and spirit to willingly submit to that will. As we grow in our love for the Lord, our desires change and our hearts rest in His promises. We pray daily for the willingness to align our will with His. Praying "if it be Thy will" is not a sign of resignation but of resolution. It requires that we not expect Him to respond to our will but that rather as we grow deeply in love with Him, we desire to respond and yield to His will for us and for others. Trusting Him for His choices and wisdom gives us a peace and a joy that no man can take away.

This is how we know that we love the children of God; by loving God and carrying out his commands. This is love for God: to obey his commands. And his commands are not burdensome. (1 John 5:1-3)

Often the path of God's will is strewn with difficulties, emotional challenges and true tests of our dependence on Him. But God never said that being a part of His kingdom and doing His will would be the easy thing to do. In fact, Paul tells us in Acts 14:22, *We must go through many hardships to enter the kingdom of God.* Jesus Himself states, *"In this world you will have trouble. But take heart! I have overcome the world."* (John 16:33) But it is in those hardships that our eyes turn toward our living example, Jesus. Molded into His likeness we become worthy of being called adopted sons. *You received the spirit of sonship. And by him we cry, "Abba, Father." The Spirit himself testifies with our spirit that we are God's children. Now if we are children, then we are heirs – heirs of God and co-heirs with Christ, if indeed we share in his sufferings in order that we may also share in his glory.* (Romans 8:15-17)

Doing God's will may often prove to be the most difficult road. But the spiritual rewards know no limits. In the words of a dear friend, after enduring a time of intense trials, "I wouldn't change of day of it. The relationship I now have in the Lord is so great and no one can take that from me."

"If it is Thy will" now resonates with new-found understanding. "Align my will with Yours, Abba, Father. Hold me close to You as I seek Your will. Then give me the strength to do that will for Your glory. Amen."

3. DIGGING IN HIS WORD

Teach me to do your will, for you are my God; may your good Spirit lead me on level ground. Psalm 143:10

Accepting my position in the kingdom of God, I desire to do the will of my Father. After seeking His face in prayer, I willingly complete His work. In doing so, I discover tremendous spiritual blessings. Look up the following verses to discover some of these blessings.

1 John 3:1; John 15:16-17; Romans 8:1-2, 15-17; Ephesians 2:19-22; Colossians 1:10-14

The strength to accomplish that will is often difficult to process alone. It is during those times that I must claim the verse, *For it is God who works in you to will and to act according to his good purpose.* (Philippians 2:13) Christ, in love, not only reveals His Father's will but also grants us the faith to work it through to completion and then equips us with *every good thing for doing His will.* (Hebrews 13:21) Believing in these promises I can cry with David, *"Teach me to do your will, for you are my God."* Psalm 143:10

Prayer: Dear Father, I desire to do Your will. Open my heart to the teachings of Your Son as I grow in that understanding. Give me a spirit of trust as I rest in You for strength and guidance through Your Holy Spirit. In Your Son's name, I pray. Amen

4
THE HEAVENLY HOOK-UP
The Interceding of the Holy Spirit

Occasionally in the room, one-hundred and twenty men and women gathered. Other times, however, the prayer vigils commenced and ended with only about fifteen or twenty individuals – the eleven remaining disciples, one newly-appointed one, a few women, Mary the mother of Jesus and Jesus' brothers. Prayer proved their means of support and comfort and held them in close union during the waiting process.

Upon Jesus' command, they remained in Jerusalem for fellowship and prayer. His words rang sharply in their ears, *"Do not leave Jerusalem, but wait for the gift my Father promised, which you have heard me speak about. For John baptized with water, but in a few days you will be baptized with the Holy Spirit ... It is not for you to know the times or dates the Father has set by his own authority. But you will receive power when the Holy Spirit comes on you; and you will be my witnesses in Jerusalem, and in all Judea and Samaria, and to the ends of the earth."* (Acts 1:4-5,7-8)

Fifty days after the Sabbath of Passover week, those assembled began to celebrate the Feast of Pentecost, also called the Feast of Weeks (Deuteronomy 16:10) or the Feast of the Harvest (Exodus 23:16). While intently praying and sharing their new-found enthusiasm after Jesus' resurrection, the sound of a sudden rushing mighty wind invaded the whole house in which they prayed. Cloven tongues of fire danced on their heads. And just as the house filled with the sound of wind, so the hearts and souls of those present became filled with the power of the Holy Spirit. God's words burned in their hearts and they could no longer keep it in. Each began praising God and speaking of Him – but in languages and tongues never taught to them. The presence of the Holy Spirit not only permeated their meeting place but their hearts, minds and tongues as well. Man's mouth became God's vessel. The gospel had to be shared, in whatever ways and means He chose.

Outside the house, others heard the sound and the verbal manifestations and wondered in amazement as to its purpose and source. *"Are not all these men who are speaking Galileans? Then how is it that each of us hears them in his own native language? Parthians, Medes and Elamites, residents of Mesopotamia, Judea and Cappadocia, Pontus and Asia, Phyrgia and Pamphylia, Egypt and the parts of Libya near Cyrene; visitors from Rome...Cretans and Arabs – we hear them declaring the wonders of God in our own tongues! ... What does this mean?"* Some, however, made fun of them and said, *"They have had too much wine."* (Acts 2:7-13)

Peter, hearing their remarks, boldly stood before them with words of power from the Holy Spirit. *"Fellow Jews...These men are not drunk, as you suppose. It's only nine in the morning. No, this is what was spoken by the prophet Joel: 'In the last days, God says, I will pour out my Spirit on all people. Your sons and daughters will prophesy, your young men will see visions, your old men will dream dreams. Even on my servants, both men and women, I will pour out my Spirit in those days, and they will prophesy. I will show wonders in the heaven above and signs on the earth below...'"* (Acts 2:14-19)

Peter's message continued as he excitedly shared the gospel message of the resurrected Christ with them. In conclusion, Peter said, *"Repent and be baptized, every one of you, in the name of Jesus Christ for the forgiveness of your sins. And you will receive the gift of the Holy Spirit. The promise is for you and your children and for all who are far off – for all whom the Lord our God will call."* (Acts 2:38,39)

Because of the Spirit's overwhelming "filling" that day, about three thousand individuals committed their lives to the Risen Lord. Jesus prediction of being witnesses *to the ends of the earth* began its fulfillment.

Those in Jerusalem continued to grow and mature in their relationship through the new "Wind" and "Fire" that had invaded their lives. Miracles, boldness and unbounding love emanated from them. Especially, *they devoted themselves to the apostles' teaching and to the fellowship, to breaking of bread and to prayer.* (Acts 2:43)

The Promise Is for You

The Holy Spirit remains our gift from the Father. Jesus promised the Spirit's coming in John 14:16-17,26, *"I will ask the Father, and he will give you another Counselor to be with you forever – the Spirit of truth. The world cannot accept him, because it neither sees him nor knows him. But you know him, for he lives with you and will be in you...But the Counselor, the Holy Spirit, whom the Father will send in my name, will teach you all things and will remind you of everything I have said to you."* It's fulfillment presented itself at Pentecost and is available to all those who love Him and accept the gospel message.

Nowhere in Scripture is there a more vivid picture of the Holy Spirit in action. The outward, visible signs serve as constant reminders of the power available to us, as one of those whom the Lord our God called. The relationship we possess with the Father manifests itself through that same

Holy Spirit. The resources available through Him are beyond human comprehension.

He Teaches Us to Look up

My fingers turned purple as a result of the strong hold I maintained. I managed to grab tightly to every strong rock, every well-rooted branch. My determination alone enabled me to continue upward. "What are you doing here, Jan? Are you crazy?" I thought to myself. Afraid of heights, I never perceived climbing a cliff to be a chosen weekend adventure.

Although shaky, I managed to wedge my feet snugly into ridges, rocky ledges and protruding rocks. About halfway up, I made the mistake of looking down. My stomach immediately became queasy and dizziness surfaced. I nearly froze in place.

"Now what do I do?" I mused. "I can't stop here. What would my boys think if their mother, who promised to take them rock climbing, freaked out?"

My friends from below must have noticed my predicament. Someone shouted, "Look up, Jan. Only look up!"

I determined to follow their instructions. Forging ahead, I completed my climb, thankful for the advice to "look up, only look up."

Grasping the reality of the power of the Holy Spirit in my life, I can only wallow in the knowledge that He alone gives me the strength to look up. When mired in self-pity, when despondent or lonely, when angered or frightened, He cries in my spirit, "Jan, look up. Seek the Lord who loves you beyond all measure. Seek those heavenly things and rest the areas of care and concern into His loving, everlasting arms."

When in emotional darkness after my first husband's death, I often found it impossible to cry out, even in prayer. At times, I would lay on the bed, void of any words. But deep in my soul, I sensed another grieving for me.

Searching Scriptures, I discovered a verse that I believe describes my experience. *In the same way, the Spirit helps us in our weakness. We do not know what we ought to pray for, but the Spirit himself intercedes for us with groans that words cannot express.* (Romans 8:26) In my mourning process, I could not verbalize the pain I experienced. But my Comforter, my Friend, my Guide, interceded for me with His own groans. His compassion for me consumed Him and I felt that compassion deep within me. I shall never forget the gratitude I felt, knowing He upheld me during that extremely difficult time.

The Wind

At the first Pentecost, the presence of the Holy Spirit manifested itself by the sound of a rushing, mighty wind. How appropriate that the Wind, which arrived after much praying and waiting, would be the generator of power for us in our prayer life. Not only would He groan for us and intercede for us, but He would reveal God's will to us as we pray. *And he who searches our hearts knows the mind of the Spirit, because the Spirit intercedes for the saints in accordance with God's will.* (Romans 8:27)

After putting on the full armor of God in Ephesians 6, Paul encourages us one step further; *And pray in the Spirit on all accasions with all kinds of prayers and requests. With this in mind, be alert and always keep on praying for all the saints.* (Ephesians 6:18) While praying "in the Spirit" may mean different things to different individuals, I begin my prayers by acknowledging how deeply I need Him. Using the Holy Spirit, the "Wind," as my guide and companion, I realize that I am no longer dependent on myself or hindered by my own inadequacies. I must remain united with the One who knows my heart, God's heart and God's will. Even when

I fail in my prayer life, He covers my mistakes by interceding. How can I lose?

The Fire

The tongues of fire that settled on the disciples heads did not consume them physically. Resting gently on the crown of their heads, it served as demonstrations of the fire burning within them. In Scripture, that sense of inward burning occurred before. The disciples who met Jesus on the road to Emmaus stated after His departure from their presence, *"Were not our hearts burning within us while he talked with us on the road and opened Scriptures to us?"* (Luke 24:32) Immediately after, they rushed to Jerusalem to tell the other disciples the exciting news.

The prophet Jeremiah said, *But if I say, "I will not mention him or speak any more in his name,' his word is in my heart like a fire, a fire shut up in my bones. I am weary of holding it in; indeed, I cannot."* (Jeremiah 20:9) His message continued as He shared God's truths to Israel.

When we are "on fire" for the Lord, we cannot be held back. His word must be shared. This became evident on Pentecost. The gospel message could not be contained in their hearts. It spilled from their lips as their shared the wonders of God in languages unknown to them.

Through the Holy Spirit, God can set our hearts on fire. Words – words in prayer – led by that Spirit, can set the world "on fire." Our cooperation with the Spirit in prayer, who alone knows the Father's will, enables change to take place. It happens, not because we have brought it about alone, but because, in seeking God's will through His Spirit, we are praying as God would want us to pray. Things will happen, when prayed in accordance with His will. *This is the confidence we have in approaching God: that if we ask anything according to his will, he hears us. And if we know that he hears us – whatever we ask – know that we have what we asked of him.* (1 John 5:14,15)

Perfect Peace

Thou will keep him in perfect peace, whose mind is stayed on thee, because he trust in thee. (Isaiah 26:3, RSV)
I prefer the RSV version of this verse because of the use of the word "stayed." As I remain fastened, glued, attached to the Holy Spirit, my life changes into the likeness of Christ. My desires become more heavenly. My will yearns to do the Father's will. My bridegroom, Jesus, permeates my spirit as I am drawn to Him. A deep sense of awareness develops as I slowly comprehend the intense price He paid for my salvation. Praise elevates and whining evaporates. The Spirit, whose purpose it is to testify of Jesus and to draw me to Him, rejoices in my victories. With the Spirit as my divine connection, peace surfaces, a peace that no one can remove. As Paul states in Romans 8:5,6, *...those who live in accordance with the Spirit have their minds set on what the Spirit desires...the mind controlled by the Spirit is life and peace.*

Remember always – *the one who is in you is greater than the one who is in the world.* (1 John 4:4) Claim it! Believe it! Live it!

4. DIGGING INTO HIS WORD

(Jesus said), *"And I will ask the Father and he will give you another Counselor to be with you forever – the Spirit of truth...he lives with you and will be in you."* (John 14:16-17)

Jesus knew that His physical presence on earth would hinder the coming of the Holy Spirit in power and in might. Granting Christ's followers the ability to serve mightily for Him, the Holy Spirit's greatest inner asset would be love. The following verses reveal that love.

Romans 5:5; Ephesians 1:18-23; Ephesians 3:14-19; Ephesians 5:1; 1 John 4:7-13

Remembering Jesus description and display of ultimate love – *"Greater love has no one than this, that he lay down his life for his friends."* (John 15:13) We rely on His Spirit to create in us that same love. As we seek the Father's will and a Christ-like character through prayer may we acknowledge and rely on the Holy Spirit who is with us and in us.

Prayer: Holy Spirit, revive my spirit today with Your presence. Create in me a willingness to listen as You guide, lead and direct me through this journey called life. Thank You for Your ever-living, ever-loving presence. Amen

5
A BRAVE WOMAN
Finding Healing in His Touch

The crowded street appears to be a perfect location for anonymity. Cloistered most of her life, she knew Jesus to be her last resort, her only hope. Others called her unclean. No one touched her. Even the law banned her from the temple, from fellowship with others and from her own close family. Her disease, an issue of blood or constant menstrual bleeding, branded her as an embarrassment, an outcast.

The law states, *When a woman has a discharge of blood for many days at a time other than her monthly period, or has a discharge that continues beyond her period, she will be unclean, just as in the days of her period. Any bed she lies on while her discharge continues will be unclean, as is her bed during her monthly period, and anything she sits on will be unclean, as during her period. Whoever touches them will be unclean; he must wash his clothes and bathe with water, and he will be unclean till evening.* (Leviticus 15:25-27)

Twelve years of loneliness preceded this moment. Visits to doctors, with every known treatment practiced, failed to bring an end to her condition. All her money vanished trying to effect a cure. Friends ignored her. Men avoided her for all would become infected and require cleansing if contact was made. Desperation seized her. In her heart she risked, not only touching those in the crowd, but touching the Priest, the Teacher, the Master Jesus. *"If I just touch his clothes, I will be healed."* she thought. (Mark 5:28)

Approaching from the rear so as to remain as unobtrusive

as possible, she inches closer and closer. Quickly and quietly, she touches the hem, the precious hem of His garment. Instantly His power flows into her and her bleeding stops. In her body, she recognizes full healing and a release from her suffering.

Embarrassment, however, proves inescapable. Startling to her ears, she hears Jesus say, *"Who touched My clothes?"* (Mark 5:30) Unable to speak at that point, others around her deny touching Him. The disciples gaze around the pressing crowd and wondered at the Master's comment. *"You see the people crowding against you...and yet you can ask, 'Who touched me?'"* (Mark 5:31) Not understanding the immense surge of power released from His very being, they look at the event realistically.

Jesus, understanding their inability to comprehend the circumstances, said, *"Someone touched me; I know that power has gone out from me."* (Luke 8:46)

Trapped, the woman inches her way around Jesus. Unable to go unnoticed any longer, she accepts her responsibility to admit the truth. Fear engulfs her as she faces the very man, the Jewish Priest, who healed her. Trembling before Him, she falls at His feet in complete submission. Jesus, who for one moment had been her sure refuge, now appears to be her accuser. Tears flow as she pours out her story of sorrow and grief.

To her surprise, the Master's gentle voice and compassionate eyes respond favorably. He not only understands her sadness and pain over the previous twelve years, but also recognizes faith in her heart. Her need and desire is not only physical but also spiritual.

"Daughter, your faith has healed you. Go in peace." He says, announcing healing in both realms. (Mark 5:34) She would not only be freed from her suffering physically but in her entire life. Peace would be her reward. She would no longer see herself as an outcast by Him or by others as a

result of her "issue of blood."

Our "Issue of Blood"

Sin – that ugly word – looms before us. As part of our nature since Adam, we struggle with that "issue of blood" daily. We try to escape it or sneak around it. In some cases, it may even cause us to be an outcast. Others cannot relieve us from its clutches or eliminate its hold in our lives. But there is One on whom we can focus that will effect a cure. His presence in our lives heals us, restores us, erases the terrible "issue of blood"– sin. We need only to cry to Him for forgiveness. In prayers of confession and surrender, we touch the sacred hem of His garment. *If we confess our sins, he is faithful and just and will forgive us our sins and purify us from all unrighteousness.* (1 John 1:9)

As the power of His Holy Spirit surges within us, we become new creatures. Clothed in the righteousness of Jesus Christ, we can accept our freedom from sin. Our "issue of blood" no longer exists. *By His wounds* (stripes, beatings, torture, agony in hell on the cross), *we are healed* (of sin, of selfishness). (Isaiah 53:4,5, parenthesis mine) His work is complete, immediate and for eternity.

"Touching His Hem" Today

Needing restoration, I grieved. No one seemed able to fill the void I experienced. I clung to the fact that the Father loved me but agonized inside over the loss of spirit that I felt. After the deaths of three special men in my life in a one year period – my last living grandfather, my husband and my father – comfort seemed so far away. Although reading Scripture proved difficult, I managed to open my Bible to Luke 8:40-48. Feeling alone, like the woman in the story, I read and reread the recording of her healing several times. I not only marveled at the love of Jesus but at the determination of the woman.

Touching His hem became her only goal. Her affliction, her loneliness and her trust in Jesus enabled her to move forward. Healing could only be effective through Him. With healing complete, Jesus, in tenderness, assured her of her healing, not only of body but of spirit. "Go in peace." he said. "Go in peace."

In tears and desperation, I cried, "Jesus, just let me touch the hem of Your garment. You have given me the privilege of prayer and now I'm claiming that "touch of Your hem" as I rest in You. I don't understand what is happening. I don't like it. But I do know that I cannot make it without You. Give me the power this woman received and help me believe a healing inside will take place."

That night as I lay in bed crying and sobbing, I sensed a need to hold Jesus' hand. While unable to do so physically, I could do so spiritually. Looking at the chair sitting next to my bed, I prayed, "Dear Jesus, I know You are there. I desire to touch You and hold Your hand." With that, I rested my hand on the chair next to me. Immediately, the crying ceased. A warmth surrounded me and peace overcame the grief. I knew He was holding my hand.

The difficult times did not end that night. Many more months of pain and grief swept over me, but when I really needed Him, He remained true. And I understood that whatever I would go through, He would be as gentle as possible. *"Come to me, all you who are weary and burdened, and I will give you rest. Take my yoke upon you and learn from me, for I am gentle and humble in heart, and you will find rest for your souls. For my yoke is easy and my burden is light."* (Matthew 11:28-30)

Coming to Him

Coming to Him in prayer, that is, touching the hem of His

garment, always effects a cure. Now I say that with all caution since there are many of you out there praying for physical healing but perhaps receiving none. You may believe that God does not hear you or your pleas for healing. But I can assure that He does hear and He does answer.

Before my first husband died, we encountered many months of severe testing. For two years, he possessed no accurate knowledge of his condition. We placed him in seven hospitals, eleven different times. While diagnosed with a rare liver disorder, his complications and symptoms appeared different than the "norm." So doctor after doctor diagnosed, probed, operated and evaluated. No real answers. People offered prayers all over the nation. Elders of the church anointed him with oil. The faith of my son, Trevin, held fast, believing with "high hopes" that his daddy would be healed. But Tom died anyway. Do I believe the Lord didn't hear our prayers? No. Do I believe there wasn't enough faith? No, definitely not. Trevin possessed enough faith for all of us. But *inner* healing did remain a constant in Tom's life during the entire ordeal.

While sometimes showing obvious signs of fear and discomfort, it never lasted long. The peace that surrounded him shone radiantly. No complaint ever came from his mouth. And his ministry to others never ceased. In hospitals, at home, with friends, he maintained secure in his trust of the Risen Savior and constantly shared it with others. With that ministry completed, God took him to His throne in heaven. What better reward could he receive!

What about my struggles? Was God not listening when pleading for a release from the emotional pain? Couldn't there have been immediate inner healing for me? I knew that God's goodness far surpassed understanding and I claimed His promises in Proverbs 3:5,6 – *Trust in the Lord with all your heart and lean not on your own understanding; In all your ways acknowledge him, and he will make your paths straight.*

As months rolled by, so did my love for an eternal, loving Father. Encountering intense grief and loneliness, I more readily understood the brutal suffering and loneliness Jesus endured. Abidingly comforted in my spirit, I recognized the role of the Holy Spirit in my life. I needed that time for growth. Through it, I discovered the eternal God in ways beyond comprehension. I not only loved Him but I was in love. I accepted Him not only in mind, but in spirit. I soon recognized that all disease, whether physical, emotional, mental or spiritual, would be used to make me more Christ-like – to be conformed in His image and to radiate His goodness. What greater answer could I receive! My first reward was spiritual. The physical remained secondary. The physical healing would have been temporary, the spiritual – eternal.

Seeking God through difficulties enables the Holy Spirit to do a good work in us. (See Philippians 1:4-6) His offer to "touch the hem of His garment" continues today. Healing takes place – maybe not always in the way we desire or expect, but in His gentle, loving way. We can rest in His abiding love as we *draw near to God, with a sincere heart in full assurance of faith, having our hearts sprinkled to cleanse us from a guilty conscience and having our bodies washed with pure water. Let us hold unswervingly to the hope we profess, for he who promised if faithful.* (Hebrews 10:22,23)

5. DIGGING INTO HIS WORD

As Jesus felt His power released with the brave woman's touch, that same power continues to be released to us through the avenue of prayer. As we touch the hem of His garment in communication, it matters not what our circumstances or "issues" are. Inner cleansing and healing will take place. The exciting promise – He will take delight in us, quiet us with His love and – can you believe it – *rejoice* over us with *singing*!

God desires and delights in our presence at His throne in heaven. Read the following verses to discover His heart of love as we seek Him.

Isaiah 57:15; Isaiah 62:5; Psalm 84:11; Psalm 86:3-7; Psalm 97:11,12; Psalm 119:58

In John 4:14, Jesus describes His gift of grace as overflowing – *"whoever drinks the water I give him will never thirst. Indeed, the water I gave him will become in him a spring of water willing up to eternal life."*

His response to us in prayer is bubbling, vigorous, "welling up." While not always immediate, it is always eternal. Relish in that goodness.

Prayer: Dear Jesus, our heart earnestly desires to experience Your power and presence through prayer. As we touch the hem of Your garment one day at a time, remind us that You take delight in our presence. May our desire to spend time with You reflect that same love and joy in return. Amen

6
AN UNTOUCHABLE OUTCAST
"Am I Worthy?"

The dampness of the cave wreaked with the smell of rotting flesh. Figures roamed inside, many covered from head to foot with cloths that showed signs of oozing sores. Stubs for hands and feet appeared as they reached to pick up food nearby. The pain they encountered found no relief as those present slowly watched each other die a slow death. Although these people were together, their loneliness proved evident. Solitude satisfied their embarrassment and shame. Not only plagued with an incurable physical condition, they also faced a life similar to those already dead, and remained banished from human society. There remained no recourse for those infected with the disease of leprosy.

One man dared venture out of this cave. Wrapped in torn clothes, his hair unkempt, this man cried out to passers-by, "Unclean, unclean." Being ceremonially unclean by God's law (Leviticus, chapters 13 & 14) required existing in this intolerable state and circumstances. Yet this man remained determined as he moved closer and closer to Jesus. His eyes and hopes remained focused on seeking help from the only person who could heal him of this incurable disease. Remaining six feet away, as the law required, he fell to his knees and cried out, *"Lord, if you are willing, you can make me clean."* (Matthew 8:2)

His voice reflected no tone of anger or insistence. In his heart, he realized his unworthiness. But his trust in Jesus' healing power motivated him to beseech his help. His words "if you are willing" manifested a heart of submission and humility. He knew it was not "owed to him" or could be demanded of Jesus. He just knew that Jesus, in His love and power, could heal him if it remained as part of His own will.

Seeing the disheveled and disease-riddled body, Jesus' heart and soul *"filled with compassion."* Knowing that coming in contact with this man meant sure death, he moved forward in love in spite of it and *"reached out his hand and touched the man."* With tenderness in His eyes, Jesus spoke.*"I am willing,"* he said. *"Be clean!"* (Mark 1:41)

Unable to believe the response, the man marveled at the words. In his spirit, he accepted the tenderness Jesus offered. In his body, he sensed amazing changes take place. As he looked down, his sores disappeared. His hands and feet returned to normal. An immediate transformation took place. The joy he experienced overwhelmed him.

Sensing his desire to shout his healing from the rooftops, Jesus requested, *"See that you don't tell this to anyone."* (Mark 1:44)

What a strange request from the Master Healer! How could one not share the excitement and enthusiasm of such a miraculous healing. Perhaps Jesus feared too much notoriety. Rather than be seen as the atoning priest, the healer from sin on the cross, He would be desired simply for His physical healing. Being sought as an earthly ruler might become the priority of others, which He did not want, for His kingdom was a spiritual kingdom, to be sought in spiritual ways.

But His desire for completion of the healing of leprosy as based on the law moved Jesus to further respond, *"But go, show yourself to the priest and offer the sacrifices that Moses commanded for Your cleansing, as a testimony to them."* (Mark 1:43) A ritual by the man, in combination with the priests (Leviticus 14), needed to be followed in the temple. Only then could his healing be accepted by God and by others.

Unable to contain himself, the man, refusing to listen to

Jesus' first plea for silence, freely spread the news everywhere he went. The Master Healer cured his incurable disease – something only God could do. The willing touch of Jesus, true God, changed the unworthy to one worthy of His love and healing.

The Leprosy of Sin

Filled with the stench of sin on the cross, the Father turned His back on His only Son, Jesus. Although having never sinned, living the law perfectly, Jesus carried a burden of sin so disgusting, that rejection of the One He held closest was certain. In so doing, every sin done by every individual throughout every generation was conquered, paid for, atoned. By our acceptance of the price paid on that cross, our sin-covered life stands erased and replaced with His righteousness. Christ, the sinless, covered Himself with the incurable leprosy of sin so that we, the sinful (the leper), might claim healing. The price has been paid by the blood of the Sacrificial Lamb. The victory has been won!

Am I Worthy?

"It's my fault. It's my fault that Jesus died on that cross. How can I ever read Scripture again? The guilt I feel rests so heavily on me. I don't even know how to pray. I am in a pit that I can't get out of. Help me, God. Please help me!"

Emotionally I sat at the bottom of an empty pit with slippery sides all around. Only a small light seemed to stream from the opening. Staring at that ray of light, of hope, I sobbed in silence. Unable to help myself, I had to trust the light to reveal a way out.

Each day I painfully waited for God, my Hope, to reveal Himself. "God, if You're real, help me to find You. Let me know that I am not a worm, a stench to you. I have no where to go but up. You alone can help me move in that direction."

My cries, buoyed by the prayers of friends and family, fell before the throne of grace. Recommended books for emotional stress, Christian friends, prayers and finally searching Scriptures revived my drowning spirit. God's light became brighter each day.

His faithfulness and goodness emerged as hope regained a stronger and stronger foothold. His presence and power became alive and, in time, I realized that my stench, my leprosy of sin, had already been cleansed. I could approach Him again, not because I was worthy, but because He was worthy and true to His promises. *Come near to God and he will come near to you...Humble yourselves before the Lord, and he will lift you up.* (James 4:8,10)

Driving in my van one day, I dwelled on 1 John 4:16. *And so we know and rely on the love God has for us. God is love. Whoever lives in love lives in God, and God in Him.* Trying to understand its meaning, I envisioned God living in me and me living in Him. Suddenly a warmth and peace settled in my spirit and I thought, "There is no where I can go that You aren't there. I am always present with You and You are always present with me. It is not dependent on who I am. It is solely dependent on Your love, especially the love reflected on the cross of Calvary."

The realization that God held me closely and tenderly, even during my emotional brokenness, overwhelmed me. Psalm 139, which I had studied earlier that week, came to mind. *You hem me in – behind and before; you have laid your hand upon me. Such knowledge is too wonderful for me, too lofty for me to attain. Where can I go from your Spirit? Where can I flee from your presence? If I go up to the heavens, you are there; if I make my bed in the depths, you are there. If I rise on the wings of the dawn, if I settle on the far side of the sea, even there your hand will guide me, your right hand will hold me fast.* (verses 5-10)

Through my search of God through Scriptures, I recognized the fact that God loves me, exactly the way I am. There is nothing I can do to make Him love me more and nothing I can do to cause Him to love me less. He accepts me exactly the way I am. Because I am a chosen child of God, I possess the privilege and honor of approaching Him. In fact, He desires my fellowship every day.

He Understands Our Weaknesses

Jesus, the true High Priest, entered the Holy of Holies in heaven offering His sacrificial blood in our stead. It came with high price. Not only did He endure the sufferings in the garden, the trial, the beatings and torture, and the cross but His entire life was plagued with every test, trial and temptation known to man.

He experienced it all – rejection, rebellion, physical and mental anguish, heartbreak from within the family and without, strain of temptation, hunger, thirst, burden of sin, to only mention a few. If I experience those same difficulties, He understands. Yet His love is unconditional, for with complete repentance (which includes a turning away), also comes full and complete forgiveness. Being His child qualifies me to serve Him, to love Him and to serve and love others for *how great is the love the Father has lavished on us, that we should be called children of God! And that is what we are!* (1 John 4:9,10)

6. DIGGING INTO THE WORD

The depth of King David's sin surpassed any he previously committed. Enticed by Bathsheba's beauty and tempted by the availability of her presence, he succumbed to the act of adultery and murder.

Confronted with his sin by the prophet Nathan, David grieved over his failure and weakness. Psalm 51 reflects his anguish and repentance. If any felt unworthy – it was David.

Read these portions of Psalm 51 and write a time that it reflects your own personal feelings.

Prayer for mercy - verses 1,2

Prayer for cleansing - verses 7,9

Prayer for a renewed spirit - verse 10

Prayer for restoration of His Holy Spirit - verses 11,12

Prayer for acceptance of a penitent heart - verse 17

Often struck by my own humanness, pleading for God's grace, I understand with Paul that *I know that nothing good lives in me, that is, in my sinful nature. For I have the desire to do what is good, but I cannot carry it out.* Romans 7:18

How frustrating! In my sinful nature, it appears hopeless. Then what chance do I have? Look up the following verses to discover our solution.

Romans 7:24,25; 2 Corinthians 3:17,18; 2 Corinthians 5:17,21; Ephesians 2:8,9

Praise God for *therefore, there is now no condemnation for those who are in Christ Jesus, because through Christ Jesus the law of the Spirit of life set me free from the law of sin and death. For what the law was powerless to do in that it was weakened by the sinful nature, God did by sending his own Son in the likeness of sinful man to be a sin offering.* (Romans 8:1-3)

Prayer: Abba Father, as I recognize my own humanity, I praise You even more for Your gift of righteousness. Through Your Son Jesus, I am set free from all that makes me unworthy. In Christ and only in Him is the cleansing complete. Thank You, Holy Father. Amen

7
THE PLEADING FATHER
Overcoming Unbelief Through Prayer

The mountain top experience overwhelmed Peter, James and John. Jesus' transfiguration filled their minds with awe and wonder. Jesus' face shone as the sun and His clothes glistened white as though washed in fuller's soap. There before them stood Elijah and Moses talking to Jesus. Suddenly a voice from heaven said, *"This is my Son, whom I love. Listen to him!"* (Mark 9:7) Wrapped in the warmth of the experience, they knew they stood on holy ground. Surely, they would find it difficult to return from the mountain. But Jesus knew they could not remain. They must travel back to the valley where hurt, pain and confusion existed and love needed to be revealed.

Reality struck the disciples quickly upon their return. Discovering the remaining nine disciples in a argument with teachers of the law, Jesus and the three disciples approached the crowd. Astonished to see Jesus, possibly still white and radiant from His mountain top experience, many rushed to His side to greet him.

Knowing a disagreement had just taken place, Jesus asked, *"What are you arguing with them about?"* (Mark 9:16)

With neither the disciples nor the teachers of the law volunteering information, a man in the crowd came forward and knelt at Jesus' feet. Feeling hopeless after the disciples' attempt to heal his demon-filled son, he begged for Jesus' help. He cried, *"Teacher, I brought you my son, who is possessed by a spirit that has robbed him of speech. Whenever it seizes him, it throws him to the ground. He foams at the mouth, gnashes his teeth and becomes rigid. I asked your disciples to drive out the spirit, but they could not."* (Mark 9:17,18)

Recognizing unbelief in the disciples and in the crowds, Jesus experienced grief and despair. He had previously commissioned and empowered the disciples to work miracles. He taught the teachers of the law and sat with the crowds on the mountain sides and on the seashore. Yet none had the faith to understand the key to unlocking God's power. With frustration mounting, He chides those present, *"O unbelieving generation...how long shall I stay with you? How long shall I put up with you? Bring the boy to me."* (Mark 9:19)

While the people seemingly failed to acknowledge the reality of Jesus' power, the demon immediately recognized the Son of God and caused the young boy to fall to the ground in convulsions. Foam spilled from the boy's mouth. Watching the boy, Jesus' heart filled with compassion. *"How long has he been like this?"* He asked. (Mark. 9:21)

Sensing the ache in Jesus' heart, the man responded, "He has been in this condition since his childhood. The demon sometimes holds such a tight grip on my son that he is cast into the fire or water in hopes of killing the boy. Jesus, I know you can do all things. If you can, please have pity on me and my son and heal him. Remove the torture of body and spirit that has inflicted him so long."

Looking at the boy's father, Jesus repeated the father's phrase, *"If you can?"* (Mark 9:23). He seemed to say, "Don't you understand yet? I have all power. I am always able to heal."

Knowing the father's spiritual condition also held an inability to fully believe in Jesus' power, He continued, *"Everything is possible for him who believes."* (Mark 9:23)

Touching the Hem of His Garment

Crying out in a pleading, piercing voice, the man said, "(Jesus), *I do believe; help me overcome my unbelief!"* (Mark 9:24, parenthesis added)

The man understood in the depths of his soul that even the power to believe came from Christ. In the agony of heart and absence of faith, he affirmed that the Giver of all faith and power needed acknowledgment.

Upon that cry for faith, Jesus demanded the demon to leave the boy's body. Violently the boy convulsed. Appearing limp and lifeless like a corpse, many thought him to be dead. But Jesus, grasping the boy's hand, lifted him up to freedom and a release from his life of agony and possession.

Later the disciples, confused and embarrassed by their inability to heal the boy, asked Jesus, *"Why couldn't we drive it out?"* (Matt. 17:19) They had previously been given the *authority to drive out evil spirits and to heal every disease and sickness*, yet their efforts proved unfruitful. (Matt. 10:1) What had they done wrong? Nine men made attempts to cast out the demon. Nine men failed.

Understanding their weakness and their lack of knowledge, Jesus responded, *"Because you have so little faith. I tell you the truth, if you have faith as small as a mustard seed, you can say to this mountain, 'Move from here to there' and it will move. Nothing will be impossible for you."* (Matt. 17:20) *"This kind can only come out with prayer and fasting."* (Mark 9:21, Amplified Bible)

A mountain faced them when they encountered this boy. Forgetting to embrace the power of God through prayer and fasting, they sought to trust in their own power – thus their downfall. The divine connection had been severed and needed to be restored if their ministry was to be successful. Seeking God's will and power needed to be utmost in their minds, a fact they had forgotten.

This Matter of Unbelief

Jesus replied, "I tell you the truth, if you have faith and do not doubt, not only can you do what was done to the fig tree, but also you can say to this mountain, 'Go throw yourself into the sea', and it will be done. If you believe, you will receive whatever you ask for in prayer." (Matthew 21:21,22)

The fig tree wasn't bearing fruit. It no longer served its purpose. Jesus knew the lesson value of the tree and chose to use it to open up the will of God. Not only did it serve as an example of what could happen to those things that are useless, but Christ Jesus used it to reveal the power of prayer and the effects of using prayer to accomplish God's will.

Nothing is too hard for God. When doing the Father's will in our lives, unbelief is often a deterrent. It stifles the imagination of God's heart and crimps the potential that His power can reveal through our prayers. In the initial story, a healing could not take place because the disciples, the members of the crowd and the father possessed a lack of faith. They chose to heal through their own means and on their own power. The power of Christ to heal the young man needed to be unleashed through prayer preparation. Determining the Father's will, seeking the power from the Son, and believing through the Spirit lacked an appearance.

Praying for Peanuts

Someone once said, "You can pray for peanuts, if it is to be used to do God's will." When praying according to the Father's will, unbelief should not be an issue. He has promised to provide and answer those prayers. Doubt should be banished. Trusting His Spirit to guide and lead us in our prayers is imperative. Our divine connection must always be intact.

We are called from a heavenly kingdom to do God's work. In His word He says, *For we are God's workmanship, created in Christ Jesus to do good works, which God prepared in advance for us to do.* (Ephesians 2:10) But only the Father in heaven fully understands what our purpose in this life holds. Through the Spirit, His will is revealed. In faith we respond to that Spirit by *doing the good works, which God prepared in advance for us to do.* It is then that we can claim the promises in John 15. *"If you remain in me and my words remain in you, ask whatever you wish, and it will be given you. This is to my Father's glory, that you bear much fruit, showing yourselves to be my disciples...You did not choose me, but I chose you and appointed you to go and bear fruit – fruit that will last. Then the Father will give you whatever you ask in my name."* (verses 7-8,16)

God's Ways Are Beyond Understanding

God's eternal purpose in our lives often remain obscured from view. Seeing through a glass dimly, we perceive His love as that of giving us everything we want. Yet His love flows much deeper than our understanding. Believing prayer is not dependent on our wants. It is dependent on His faithfulness – His goodness – His kindness – His compassion. Believing prayer is trusting Him so much that we praise Him for the strength He supplies *through the valley of the shadow of death.* (Psalm 23:4) It is the acceptance of fear without understanding, yet trudging forward while holding the hand of the Holy One, Jesus Christ. Knowing that tribulation and suffering develop Christ's character in us, we yield our lives to Him and offer our *sacrifice of praise.* (Hebrews 13:15)

Can unbelief hinder prayer? Absolutely! Is unanswered prayer always a sign of unbelief? Absolutely not! Deep in the heart of God rests the eternal purpose for each of us. No one dare tread on Holy Ground to assume we know Him well enough to provide the answers to all concerns. Use Job as an example. How often he and his friends tried to determine the cause of the terrible calamities in his life, yet none could know the heavenly battle that had ensued with Satan. When God finally confronted Job, He made no excuses or explanations – no justification. He was God, the great "I AM" and that was enough. With that realization, Job finally answered the Lord, *"I am unworthy – how can I reply to you? I put my hand over my mouth"* (Job 40:4) *"I know that you can do all things; no plan of yours can be thwarted. You asked, 'Who is this that obscures my counsel without knowledge?' Surely I spoke of things I did not understand, things too wonderful for me to know."* (Job. 42:2,3)

Beware of Assumptions

Often assumptions are made regarding God's will for another individual. Without meaning to, attacks are made on those who are already going through emotionally difficult times.

One such situation occurred to me several years after Tom died. Upon discussing briefly the circumstances of Tom's death in a Sunday morning Bible class, a man approached me immediately. Firmly believing in "faith healing", he said, "Jan, if you had only had enough faith, your husband would not have died."

Having prayed and agonized over this approach before, I responded with words only the Spirit could have given me. "You know, you may be right. But if Tom's healing was dependent on faith, my son, Trevin, held enough for both of us. He did not waver in his belief that his daddy would get well. But Tom died anyway. Now we both hold tightly to the knowledge that God removed his father from us because his ministry on earth was finished and that God, our loving

Father, possessed an eternal purpose we have yet to recognize. In the meantime, we are moving onward to bigger and greater things for God. But Tom's memory will forever touch our hearts as we remember a deeply spiritual man who displayed God's love constantly. What greater legacy could he have left his family and others!"

Much guilt has been heaped on grieving people by the thoughtless quotes – "You know it was God's will." or "If only you had possessed enough faith, your loved one would have been healed."

Who are we to presume we know God's will for another individual? Did we seek God regularly in prayer? Did we approach the throne of grace and pray for wisdom from the Spirit in knowing how to pray? Many have left the church because of careless words. As you draw closer to Jesus Christ, pray for a spirit of understanding and gentleness so that careless words may not cause another to reject what God desires.

If I have learned anything over the years, it is that God's everlasting arms and tender compassion are ever-available. As I cry out to God, He grants me faith even in the midst of wavering moments and my "pits." What comfort it is to know that my faith rests in the loving arms of the Savior who willingly gave His life for me. As I plead, "Help my unbelief," He responds, "I already have!"

7. Digging into His Word

Because of the Lord's great love we are not consumed, for his compassions never fail. They are new every morning; great is your faithfulness. I say to myself, "The Lord is my portion; therefore I will wait for him." Lamentations 3:22-24

As I look back on my past, I realize that I missed out on numerous experiences in life because of unbelief. Fear dominated over faith and the need to remain in my "comfort zone" dug deeply. As I approach maturity, I discover a release from those shackles that once bound me. While symptoms of unbelief still trickle in, I find it easier to cry out to the Holy Spirit for faith. As I seek refuge in Him, He restores me and enables me to go on the heights.

Read the following verses to discover the source of faith and its blessings.

Psalm 37:39-40; Psalm 40:1-3; Psalm 52:8; Psalm 55:16-18; Isaiah 40:29; Isaiah 41:9-10; Habakkuk 3:19

Write Lamentations 3:25,26 as a reminder of the rewards of waiting for His goodness to be revealed.

Prayer: Holy Spirit, my life ebbs and flows with pain and pleasure, abundance and strife, joy and sorrow. In my good times and bad, remind me of the need to stay close to the vine – Jesus Christ. Grant me the faith I need to seek to be like Him. In His name I pray. Amen

8
A Persistent Widow
Never Give Up!

His parables appeared profound and misunderstood. Many individuals lacked the spiritual ability to grasp the meanings and often his own disciples needed an explanation. But He loved sharing them and used them to enable his disciples to grow in strength and maturity.

One such story invited the disciples to develop their prayer life. Often delays in answered prayers caused them and others to become discouraged and lose heart. The battles, the struggles with life appeared endless and fruitless. The Master's desire to reveal the Father's love in their prayers manifested itself. In all things and at all times, the earnestness of prayer needed a boost. Giving up when confronted by the adversaries of earthly life needed to be addressed.

The disciples knew and understood the picture of an unjust judge. Since the Jews themselves were not tried by judges but by the Jewish counsels, most judges encountered by them were Romans and appointed by Herod. Often dishonest in their appropriations to others, they catered to the wealthy, affluent people who could afford them a payoff or grant them prestige by hearing their case. Seldom did a judge listen to the lower individuals, especially a widow. Time could not be wasted on the ordinary.

"Imagine," Jesus said, "a widow bravely confronting such a judge. Knowing her case to be honest and right, she expected a hearing. 'Please give me the justice I deserve against my enemy,' she pleaded.

"Day after day, she faced the judge and hounded him for mercy. Day after day, the judge refused to review her case. But her determination failed to cease. With no one else to defend her, she knew this judge to be her only hope. In her heart, she held fast and became an annoyance, a boil in the judge's life.

"In his frustration, the judge cried out, *'Even though I don't fear God or care about men, yet because this widow keeps bothering me, I will see that she gets justice, so that she won't eventually wear me out with her coming!'*" (Luke 18:4,5)

Her intolerable persistence broke the man down.

Focusing on his story, Jesus continues. *"Listen to what the unjust judge says. And will not God bring about justice for his chosen ones, who cry out to him day and night? Will he keep putting them off? I tell you, he will see that they get justice and quickly."* (Luke 18:6-8)

Turning the parable heavenward, Jesus assures the disciples that the Father in heaven not only will hear and respond to the persistent agonizing prayers of His chosen ones, but will answer speedily and without delay. As the adversaries in our lives pounce on us, the Father will lovingly respond with protection and a ready assurance of His comfort and compassion. There will not be one second that passes without His overseeing, defending hand in the picture.

Persistent Moses

"When I looked, I saw that you had sinned against the Lord your God; you had made for yourselves an idol cast in the shape of a calf. You had turned aside quickly from the way that the Lord had commanded you. So I took the two tablets and threw them out of my hands breaking them to

pieces before your eyes.

"Then once again I fell prostrate before the Lord for forty days and forty nights; I ate no bread and drank no water, because of all the sin you had committed, doing what was evil in the Lord's sight and so provoking him to anger. I feared the anger and wrath of the Lord, for he was angry enough with you to destroy you. But again the Lord listened to me. And the Lord was angry enough with Aaron to destroy him, but at that time I prayed for Aaron too...

"And when the Lord sent you out from Kadesh Barnea, he said, 'Go up and take possession of the land I have given you.' But you rebelled against the command of the Lord your God. You did not trust him or obey him. You have been rebellious against the Lord ever since I have known you.

"I lay prostrate before the Lord those forty days and forty nights because the Lord had said he would destroy you. I prayed to the Lord and said, 'O Sovereign Lord, do not destroy your people, your own inheritance that you redeemed by your great power and brought out of Egypt with a mighty hand...Overlook the stubbornness of this people, their wickedness and their sin...They are your people, your inheritance that you brought out by your power and your outstretched arm.'" (Deuteronomy 9:16-20,23-26,29)

Moses' adversary consisted of a people, over a million in number – a rebellious, discontented, grumbling nation. But rather than throw up his hands in despair, he committed himself to prayer. And it changed God's heart from anger and destruction to lesser penalties and forgiveness. What an awesome God we have! He listened to the persistent, devoted prayer of one man – a man who saved an entire nation on his knees.

Can we, the people of God, save our nation on our knees today? Have we even tried? Faced with a country on a spiritual downhill slide, our goal should hold true to pray daily and on our knees for its salvation.

"If my people, who are called by my name, will humble themselves and pray and seek my face and turn from their wicked ways, then will I hear from heaven and will forgive their sin and will heal their land. Now my eyes will be open and my ears attentive to the prayers offered in this place." (2 Chronicles 7:14,15)

It is important to note that this verse is referring to God's own people. **We** are the ones who are to humble ourselves. **We** are the chosen people who can pray and seek the face of God. **We** are the ones who are to *turn from our wicked ways.* Apathy and an inconsistent, uncommitted prayer life dominates many of our churches. It is amazing to me how many individuals with whom I come in contact have little or no prayer life. Excuses abound. But if our nation is to revive and the tides of evil change, it must begin with ourselves, the people who are called by His name. The unsaved and unredeemed can't do it – it is **our** supreme and dire responsibility.

This chapter is written less than a week after the horrible, senseless murders of twelve people at Columbine High School in Littleton, Colorado. While the mentioning of God's name is not allowed in many schools, God's love and power manifested itself. Although prayer is banned from most schools, prayer existed in the school that day. Religious services and prayer vigils abounded as people of all races and nationalities huddled together in love and comfort.

As with many others, grief surged through my very being. Having a burden for children in my own soul, I agonized, not only for those who died and their loved ones, but for the condition of our nation. What could be happening within the lives of our precious children to allow such hatred to abound! Helplessness surfaced as I wondered what the next ten or twenty years would bring. Yet I received comfort from His Spirit as I accepted the responsibility to pray more earnestly. Prayers need to be lifted daily for my children and grandchildren, those in my neighborhood, and in the schools in my city. I thought, "If only Christians around the nation would join one another in prayer for the protection, the filling of the Spirit and the unsaved in those schools, what exciting things could happen!" I now pray for a mighty army of God's people to surface – to take on this commitment in every city of every state in the entire nation. We need to save the children for it is Satan's greatest arena today – God's power through prayer must prevail against it!

Pray and Not Faint

"It is our privilege and honour that we *may* pray. It is our duty; we *ought to pray*. It is to be our constant work; we ought *always* to pray. We must pray, and never grow weary of praying, till it comes to be swallowed up in everlasting praise. But that which seems particularly designed here is to teach us constancy and perseverance in our requests for some spiritual mercies that we are in pursuit of, relating either to ourselves or to the church of God. When we are praying for strength against our spiritual enemies, our lists and corruptions, we must continue instant in prayer, must pray and *not faint*, for we shall not *seek God's face in vain.*" (1)

The adversary for God's elect crouches at the gate. Grief, financial burdens, incest, rape, wayward children, abuse, homosexuality, for example, touch the people of God as frequently as unbelievers. Today, Satan is on a rampage and those spiritual forces need to be resisted and prevailed against. *For our struggle is not against flesh and blood, but against the rulers, against the authorities, against the powers of this dark world and the spiritual forces of evil in the heavenly realms.* (Ephesians 6:12)

While some sins we fall into are the direct result of our own choice to succumb to temptations, yet others are impaled on us by the direct forces of evil. Praying for release cannot be done in a mundane manner. Rather, it takes energy, persistence and the armor of God if we are to prevail. Ephesians 6 gives us the tools of the trade to combat Satan and His forces. Because of Christ's redeeming blood, the victory is ours. Claiming His power, we hold up the belt of truth, the breastplate of righteousness, the gospel of peace, the shield of faith, the helmet of salvation and the word of God. Then we *pray in the Spirit on all occasions, with all kinds of prayers and requests.* (Ephesians 6:18)

God awarded us with the dynamics of prayer. In cooperation with the mighty Father, translated by Jesus and empowered by the Holy Spirit, we are enabled to fight the adversaries in our lives. As we cry to him day and night, He promises to hear us. As we pray with earnestness, we must be willing to wrestle with God and give him no rest until the adversary has been oppressed or unless the Spirit so leads us. Our persistence is not a nuisance to God. Rather, He beckons us to come and even engages Himself in our prayers.

Listen heartily to His voice (that means remaining quiet before Him), indulge in Scripture and obey His call to persist. When His "due time" has passed, His promise will be fulfilled. *And the God of all grace, who called you to his eternal glory in Christ, after you have suffered a little while, will himself restore you and make you strong, firm and steadfast. To him be the power for ever and ever. Amen* (1 Peter 5:10,11)

(1) Matthew Henry, *Commentary in One Volume*(Grand Rapids, MI:Zondervan, 1961), 1480

8. Digging into His Word

Therefore, since we are surrounded by such a great cloud of witnesses, let us throw off everything that hinders and the sin that so easily entangles, and let us run with perseverance the race marked out for us. Let us fix our eyes on Jesus, the author and perfecter of our faith, who for the joy set before him endured the cross, scorning its shame, and sat down at the right hand of the throne of God. Consider him who endured such opposition from sinful men, so that you will not grow weary and lose heart. Hebrews 12:1-3

This Scripture reading relates two major points needed in persistent prayer. Verse 2 states: *Let us fix our eyes on Jesus, the author and perfecter of our faith.* With our eyes focused on Jesus and His desire to create a Christ-like image in us, we rely on the promise that waiting for His response has an eternal purpose.

Look up the following verses to discover the rewards for waiting.

Psalm 27:14

Psalm 130:5-7

Isaiah 30:18

Isaiah 40:31

Verse 3 states: Do *not grow weary or lose heart.* In the throes of heartache and pain, the temptation to succumb to despair often wins. But Luke encourages us to yield to the gentle reins of Christ's love and accept his temporary discipline.

Read Hebrews 12:10-11 to discover the purpose and product of God's discipline.

Luke concludes the section in verse 12 by encouraging us with these words related to prayer. *Therefore, strengthen your feeble arms and weak knees.* Never give up, dear children, never give up!

Prayer: Dear Father, there are times when I am tempted to despair. Giving up on You and others remain a viable option. Grant me Your Spirit that, with Your strength, I may step beyond the problem to rest secure in the Problem-Solver. Thank You for Your tender, loving patience. You are truly an awesome God. Amen

9
THE CARING CENTURION
Praying For Others

Most Roman soldiers loathed slaves. If subjected to suffering, severe illness or even death, it mattered not. Considered scum, their passing would go virtually unnoticed to the Romans, especially to the centurions. They cared much more for their position and the one-hundred men under their care.

One man, however, dared to be different. Deep in his soul the centurion believed in the God of the Jews. He manifested piety and a godly lifestyle, even donating to the building of the Jewish temple in Capernaum. Now his beloved bondservant lay in bed suffering from a painful disease that would soon take his life. Seeking to find Jesus, the oft-heard-of Healer, the centurion summoned assistance from Jewish friends.

The hearts of these Jewish elders esteemed him highly. Although restricted by Rabbinical law to associate or eat with the gentiles or sinners, a bond of unique friendship existed between the centurion and this group of Jews. In their eyes, he was deserving and worthy of a hearing. Even though it was strictly forbidden for a Jew to enter a gentile home, (see John 4:9; 18:28; Acts 11:2,3 and Matthew 9:9-13) the Jewish leaders pleaded earnestly for Jesus to visit this centurion, this gentile. His love of the Jewish nation warranted a visit from the Jewish Healer. In addition, they observed a tender, compassionate heart toward his slave rarely seen among his kind.

Consenting to go, Jesus neared the centurion's home. However, before He arrived, another delegation of friends stood in the way of Jesus' upcoming entry. A message from the centurion amazes Jesus as He listens to this man's understanding of Jewish laws. In addition, respect for Jesus displays itself as the centurion refuses to allow Jesus to enter his home.

Friends share the centurion's message: *"Lord, don't trouble yourself, for I do not deserve to have you come under my roof. That is why I did not even consider myself worthy to come to you."* (Luke 7:6,7)

In spite of his position, he reflected deep, abiding humility. Beseeching the awesomeness of God Himself, this centurion recognized his own unworthiness. Before God, any goodness received displayed grace. His unworthiness did not value a visit, but his valued servant deserved a cure. Pleading his servant's cause, the centurion begs for Jesus' healing, but not by a public appearance. *"But say the word, and my servant will be healed. For I myself am a man under authority, with soldiers under me. I tell this one, 'Go', and he goes; and that one, 'Come', and he comes. I say to my servant, 'Do this', and he does it."* (Luke 7:8)

He acknowledges not only Jesus' authority to heal but displays faith and trust in Jesus' power to heal with a single word. For just as the centurion himself could command others by a word and it would happen, so Jesus could dispel the suffering and illness of his servant with the use of His word. He revealed no doubt in Jesus perfect ability to perform such an act. He knew neither space nor time could obstruct Jesus' power to heal.

Amazed at the man's deep confession of faith, Jesus turns to the crowds surrounding Him. *"I tell you, I have not found such great faith even in Israel."* (Luke 7:9) While a gentile, this man expressed a profound and pleasing faith to the Son of Man – a faith worthy of recognition.

Jesus pronounces the healing. *"Go! It will be done just as you believed it would.' And his servant was healed at that very hour."* (Matthew 8:13)

Testing Our Motives

Little two-year-old Grace searched for me with apparent frustration mounting. Unable to view my approach behind her, she kept calling, "Miss Jan, Miss Jan!" Finally I called out to her, "Grace, I'm right here." With that she spun around, threw up her hands and shouted in a relieved voice, "Miss Jan!" She bounded toward me, arms out, ready to be picked up. My heart overflowed with pride and warmth at the thought of being so deeply loved. Upon giving her a hug, she quietly responded, "Cookie!"

While I relished the hug, I admitted within that my bubble of pride popped. What I thought existed as a display of love also included a desire for the goodies I could offer.

In my own heart, I began to examine my motives for so many of my prayers of intercession. When needs and concerns fill my life and the life of others, I often begin and end (and sometimes all-include) prayers of needs, wants and desires. The prayers, fail to praise God, to express love or to thank Him for His goodness in the past. I remain focused on what I can get, rather than on the Maker who desires my love, adoration and thanksgiving. Rushing to God in prayer, I lift my hands and shout, "Gimme! Cookie!"

The most rewarding aspect of the experience remains bound in my response to Grace and also in the Father's response to me. As I continued to hug Grace, knowing the cookies had already been stored in the cabinet, I looked at her mother and asked, "Mommy, can I get her one?" My love for her far surpassed the inconvenience it would cause, as my heart desired to give her what she asked.

In the same manner, I picture Jesus hugging me saying,

"Daddy, can I get her one?" His unconditional, sacrificial love floods over the slight hurt of my lack of recognition for Him and desires to grant me my request, providing it meets with the Father's approval.

Lord, Teach Us to Pray

Observing Jesus communicate with His Father in prayer must have been an awesome experience. After one such occasion, his disciples approached Him and said, *"Lord, teach us to pray, just as John taught his disciples."* (Luke 11:1) Viewing a spirit of love and tender concern through His prayer life, their hearts must have burned within to understand that source and dynamic of power.

What followed remains the most prominent and often used prayer today – the Lord's prayer. Within those brief words exists every aspect of prayer needed to sustain our daily life and to serve as an outline for future prayers – praise, adoration, acknowledgment of His kingdom and His will, provisions for *daily* needs, forgiveness from God and the willingness to forgive others, the ability to resist the temptations and protection from the evil one. All else is secondary.

In our materialistic world today, our wants often far exceed our needs. I am reminded of the verse in James 4:3, *When you ask, you do not receive, because you ask with wrong motives, that you may spend what you get on your pleasures.* James further adds that the wrong motives cause quarreling, fighting and coveting. Selfishness, even in our prayer life, breeds dissatisfaction and a lust for more. Examining our motives in intercession heads up the list of needed meditation concerns before prayers are sent heavenward.

Jesus desires that our first concern be for *daily needs* and the kingdom's work that He opens for us. But other requests never fall on deaf ears. God's availability and willingness to listen to all requests exists. However those requests are filtered through unbounding love with an eternal purpose in mind. Some may be forfeited for the sake of the whole. Some requests appear unanswered but rest in His loving right hand for the future or for spiritual purposes. But in all these things, growth in prayer surfaces. The more we communicate, the more we grow. The more we trust Jesus to "teach us to pray", the more opportunities will arise for us to learn. In time, our communication with God exists as a daily, hourly and sometimes, even closer, event. Prayer not only becomes our life, prayer **is** our life-relationship with God.

We Cooperate with God in Prayer

Our loving heavenly Father chooses to include us in the process of prayer. While He certainly possesses all power and can alter all things on His own, yet His love for us reflects companionship and cooperation. An abundance of potential prayers go unanswered because they never formed in our hearts or on our lips. Exciting miracles remain unfinished because God's people were to busy to pray.

Prayer reflects a relationship with Him. A lack of communication may indicate a lack of love or the existence of too many distractions presented by the world. I once heard, "If you truly want a gauge of your spiritual life – check your prayer life."

Because a loving relationship forms through our sharing and communion with Him, much energy needs to be spent sitting at His throne, pleading the cause of people today. In doing so, our relationship with Him strengthens and we discover that our cooperation in prayer does effect His decisions. (Moses in chapter 8 gave witness of that.)

The new Christians in Acts upheld active prayer lives. Numbers grew and miracles happened. Look at Acts 12:5-16 for a classic example. What is so unique is that even they were stunned at the results.

So Peter was kept in prison, but the church was earnestly praying to God for him. The night before Herod was to bring him to trial, Peter was sleeping between two soldiers, bound with two chains, and sentries stood guard at the entrance. Suddenly an angel of the Lord appeared and a light shone in the cell. He struck Peter on the side and woke him up. "Quick, get up!" he said, the chains fell off Peter's wrists.

Then the angel said to him, "Put on your clothes and sandals." And Peter did so.

"Wrap your cloak around you and follow me," the angel told him. Peter followed him out of the prison, but he had no idea that what the angel was doing was really happening; he thought he was seeing a vision. They passed the first and second guard and came to the iron gate leading to the city. It opened for them by itself, and they went through it. When they had walked the length of one street, suddenly the angel left him.

Then Peter came to himself and said, "Now I know without a doubt that the Lord sent his angel and rescued me from Herod's clutches and from everything the Jewish people were anticipating."

When this had dawned on him, he went to the house of Mary the mother of John, also called Mark, where many people had gathered and were praying. Peter knocked at the outer entrance, and a servant girl named Rhoda came to answer the door. When she recognized Peter's voice, she was so overjoyed she ran back without opening it and exclaimed, "Peter is at the door!"

"You're out of your mind," they told her. When she kept insisting that it was so, they said, "It must be his angel."

But Peter kept on knocking, and when they opened the door and saw him, they were astonished.

They prayed earnestly – yet they were astonished at the

miracle! How often in life we pray for miracles, for changes, for growth and become astonished when it happens. God's mercies and goodness evidently greatly exceed our expectations. But what excitement He generates within us when it occurs. Praise Him, for His wonders never cease.

Pray for Heavenly Things

On their release, Peter and John went back to their own people and reported all that the chief priests and elders had said to them. When they heard this, they raised their voices together in prayer to God. "Sovereign Lord," they said, "you made the heaven and the earth and the sea, and everything in them...Now, Lord, consider their threats and enable your servants to speak your word with great boldness. Stretch out your hand to heal and perform miraculous signs and wonders through the name of your holy servant Jesus."
After they prayed the place where they were meeting was shaken. And they were all filled with the Holy Spirit and spoke the word of God boldly. (Acts 4:23-24, 29-31)

These men had just previously been jailed for their testimony of faith, stood before the Sanhedrin and were warned to refrain from speaking any longer in Jesus' name. Yet they didn't cower and run or even pray for a way of escape. Instead they prayed for courage and boldness. They requested a greater ability to reveal Jesus Christ to others. God granted them that prayer.

Examining my prayer life, I failed miserably to pray for open doors to witness. I filled my vision with the day's concerns and problems rather than God's vision for saving the lost. Neglecting to pray for courage, for faith, for those spiritual gifts needed to accomplish His will, I sat on the sidelines rather than participate in the joy of the event. The worst part – I was content to be there. I failed to experience God's overwhelming power in my life because of fear and a sense of inadequacy. That thought grieves me today but now I pray earnestly for the courage and determination to step out in faith. With His vision foremost in my heart and mind, prayers for myself and others include the spiritual much more than the physical.

I now encourage you to evaluate your prayer life in that light. Do most of your prayers include requests for the material, the physical? Do you include prayers for depth of faith, courage and the Spirit's power for yourself and others? Do you seek God's kingdom first in your prayer life or are more concerned about what this world can offer? Make a commitment today to pray for the spiritual more than the physical and you will see exciting things happen.

Praying with the Brethren

The new disciples devoted themselves to the apostles' teaching and to the fellowship, to the breaking of bread and to prayer. Everyone was filled with awe, and many wonders and miraculous signs were done by the apostles. (Acts 2:42,43)

These disciples not only believed in prayer; they practiced it; they encouraged it. They knew that if the prayer of a righteous man has a powerful effect, the prayer of many righteous would be dynamite. They claimed it, believed it, and used it! They chose to fight Satan, resist temptation, heal the sick, seek courage, and procure salvation – all through their Spirit-led prayers.

Praying with the brethren, for the brethren, miracles abounded. God's kingdom enlarged. The word of Jesus' salvation by grace through the cross spread like wildfire. Praising lips could not be restrained. Acknowledgment of God's power manifested itself. Jesus became a word of strength to the believer and a word of contempt to the skeptic. Yet the numbers grew day after day. The believers' cooperation with God in prayer brought amazing results.

Praying with the brethren, for the brethren, today still cradles the same power. Remembering that *Jesus Christ is the same yesterday and today and forever*, I can claim the same promise of Jesus in Matthew 18. (Hebrews 13:8) Gathering with my friends in prayer, whether in their presence, on the phone, on a chain or over the wave lengths of email, I believe that God's power reveals itself through the prayers of many righteous people. Satan needs an army of prayer warriors to resist him. To this we are called – to this we are privileged!

Just as the early Christians experienced miracles through their persistence in prayer, so many have experienced mighty miracles at His loving hand. Healings of body and soul, lives forever changed, fears dispelled, and addictions ended – only to mention a few. Intercessory prayer hugs the very essence of our life as a Christian. Cooperation with the Father, the Son and the Spirit in procuring His glory remains forever our goal as His precious children. Hold tightly to it.

9. Digging into His Word

Fearless, courageous, his heart ablaze, Paul shared the gospel with others. Although stoned, dragged out of the city and left for dead, he revived and not only continued his Christ-like goal, but returned to the same city to witness again. Prayers for those saved and churches he started, never ceased to flow from his lips – both in commissioning and committing.

Paul's life exemplified intercessory prayer as do other powerful figures in Scripture. Read the following verses and write the person who prays and for whom or what they pray.

1 Samuel 12:19-25

Daniel 2:17-19

Psalm 51:10

John 17

Acts 4:23-31

Acts 7:59-60

Acts 13:2-3

Acts 20:32-37

Ephesians 6:18-20

I Timothy 2:1-3

Hebrews 13:7

James 1:5-7

Peace that surpasses understanding is awarded those who surrender all in prayer, for Jesus promises, *"Peace I leave with you; my peace I give you. I do not give to you as the world gives. Do not let your hearts be troubled and do not be afraid."* (John 14:27) Remember – prayerful petitions procure peace.

Prayer: Jesus, in Your presence, grant us the Spirit of wisdom and guidance as we pray for the needs of others. Open our eyes to Your Father's will as we lift friends, neighbors and those we love to Your throne of grace. May their salvation and Christ-like lives always be foremost in our hearts and minds. Thank You for the freedom of prayer offered upon Your death on the cross. You are to be praised! Amen

10
A HUMBLE TAX COLLECTOR
Claiming Promises

Jesus observed it often. Standing in prominent places, faces painted white, with a haggard-look and disheveled appearance – they appeared pious and saintly. Their prayers were lengthy, their hands uplifted, and their faces drawn heavenward. To the outsider, these Pharisees upheld the epitome of godliness. No one compared and few tried.

Yet Jesus' eyes of wisdom perceive a picture that penetrates past the exterior. Inside He sees white-washed tombs. In their hearts he recognizes pride, arrogance and a need for recognition. Besides false humility, Jesus also perceives overwhelming prejudice. Trusting in their own right standing with God, they make nothing of the rest of man.

Jesus shared many parables, some difficult to interpret. But this parable lacked that aspect, for obvious truth exuded. *To some who were confident of their own righteousness and looked down on everybody else, Jesus told this parable:* (Luke 18:9)

"Picture if you will, two men committed to prayer. One is a Pharisee. The other, a publican or tax collector.

"The Pharisee prays and fasts twice weekly even though the Mosiac requirement held only a yearly fast – the Day of Atonement. Visible signs of his piety appear. Many esteem him highly for his outward sings of religion. In the public eye, a better religious man could barely exist.

"Appearing before the throne of grace in prayer (or his

form of prayer), He begins, *'God, I thank you that I am not like other men – robbers evildoers, adulterers – or even like this tax collector. I fast twice a week and give a tenth of all I get.'* (Luke 18:11,12)

"When approaching God, his confidence rests in accomplishments. Informing God of his goodness, he believes that God now owes him something in return.

"Observing the tax collector huddled in a corner of the courtyard, the proud Pharisee points to that man, that *sinner,* and expounds on his thankfulness before God that he is not like him. After all tax collectors steal money from others when collecting taxes and keep it for themselves. They become wealthy while making others poor. Not only is the man not a Pharisee but his chosen profession proves to be among the worst.

"Far away from the Pharisee, the tax collector understands his position among those he considers saintly. Positioned at an obscure location, his heart lays burdened with sin. Grieving over his choices in life and the depth of need for mercy and forgiveness, his eyes look downward. A sinner such as he deserves so little. In shame, humility, disgrace and anguish, the tax collector beats his breast. Sorrow overwhelms him. God's forgiveness faces him as his greatest need. *'God, have mercy on me, a sinner.'* (Luke 18:13)

"Fleeing to the mercy seat, he seeks a place of refuge and cleansing. His heart may have believed and claimed the promises of David in Psalm 51:7-10: *Cleanse me with hyssop, and I will be clean; wash me, and I will be whiter than snow. Let me hear joy and gladness; let the bones you have crushed rejoice. Hide your face from my sins and blot out all my iniquity. Create in me a pure heart, O God, and renew a steadfast spirit within me."*

His parable complete, Jesus faces his audience. *"I tell you that this man, rather than the other, went home justified before God. For everyone who exalts himself will be* humbled, and he who humbles himself will be exalted." (Luke 18:14)

The Pharisee, only impressing himself, received nothing from God. *A man's pride brings him low, but a man of lowly spirit gains honor.* (Proverbs 29:23).

But trusting in God's promises paid off for the tax collector. In humbleness of heart and spirit, he touched God and received forgiveness. *"This is the one I esteem: he who is humble and contrite in spirit, and trembles at my word."* (Isaiah 66:2) *"Blessed are the pure in heart, for they will see God."* (Matthew 5:8)

Standing on the Promises

Your kingdom is an everlasting kingdom, and your dominion endures through all generations. The Lord is faithful to all his promises and loving toward all he has made. (Psalm 145:13)

"I want to know this God in whom I have believed all these years. I've read about You. I learned about You in Sunday School and church. I've given my life to You over and over. Yet, there seems to be so little I know, really know, about You. Please reveal Yourself to me." A desperate void of understanding and wisdom existed. Desiring it to be filled, I prayed for doors to open.

Remembering the words of a special friend who found tremendous comfort in the Psalms, I resolved to begin there. One of the first verses I discovered is the above verse. Grasping tightly to His promises, I claimed verse after verse that touched the heart of my concerns and my need to accept and acknowledge God and His wisdom in my circumstances. Substituting or adding my name to verses, Scripture opened as a rich heritage of grace and love. A New Testament verse I quoted daily was, *"And I pray that you,* (Jan) *being rooted and established in love, may have power, together with all the saints, to grasp how wide and long and high and deep is the love of Christ, and to know this love that surpasses knowledge – that you* (Jan) *may be filled to the measure of all the fullness of God."* (Ephesians 3:17-19)

God, in His abiding love, did not disappoint me. He proved faithful to His promises as I not only discovered what "this God" is like but fell deeply in love with Him. Knowing Him as the Trinity overwhelmed and inspired me – my loving, protecting Father; my sacrificial, abiding Bridegroom Jesus; and my encouraging, comforting Spirit. Through it I learned the importance of using Scripture in prayers and continue to use it daily in my prayer life. May you discover His richness as you lean on His promises.

Promise of Cleansing and Forgiveness

Let us draw near to God with a sincere heart in full assurance of faith, having our hearts sprinkled to cleanse us from a guilty conscience and having our bodies washed with pure water. (Hebrews 10:22)

If we confess our sins, he is faithful and just and will forgive us our sins and purify us from all unrighteousness. (1 John 1:9)

During my battle with fear, Satan often inflicted me with guilt. He sought to dishearten and destroy my faith. I remembered the saying I once heard, "If you live with guilt, you show that you refuse to accept Christ's costly price on the cross."

Conviction and penitence (turning away from sin) is an act of the Holy Spirit. Guilt is a tool of Satan. Understanding that, I claimed the two verses above. While focusing on the first part of the verses for *my* participation, I prayed for the Spirit's help in drawing near to God with a sincere heart and in confessing my sin. Upon doing so, I then claimed the remainder of the verses, "Jan, He will cleanse you from a guilty conscience and wash you with pure water." "He is faithful and just and will forgive you for your sins and cleanse you from ALL unrighteousness." WOW! What an awesome freedom resulted!

And no one or nothing can take that cleansing away. *In all these things we are more than conquerors through him who love us. For I am convinced that neither death nor life, neither angels nor demons, neither the present nor the future, nor any powers, neither height nor depth, nor anything else in all creation, will be able to separate us* (including you, Jan) *from the love of God that is in Christ Jesus our Lord.* (Romans 8:37-39)

Seek Christ First

Many books are available today listing promises of God – in categories for every need. I personally would like to share four categories with you as God revealed them to me during my difficult times. But because each person's needs remain varied and personal, often God Himself must reveal the promises that fit each specific need.

As I shared with my sons and others, when searching Scripture don't seek answers – seek God. In Him you will find answers for His is *the Way, the Truth and the Life.* (John 14:6) In Him all promises are fulfilled and all needs met. As Simon Peter said in John 6:68, *"Lord, to whom shall we go? You have the words of eternal life."*

Enrich Your Prayer Life

The dynamics of praying God's promises includes first accepting our role, then praying for the Spirit's help in performing it and claiming the promise given. Below are listed Bible verses in four different areas. In several, I will add my name and the proper pronoun in parenthesis so you can better understand its use. It adds a powerful punch to believing prayer since promises, when prayed in humility and submission, *will* be answered.

1. PEACE:

Thou dost keep (Jan) *in perfect peace, whose mind is stayed on thee, because* (she) *trusts in thee.* Isaiah 26:3, RSV

The fruit of righteousness will be peace; the effect of righteousness will be quietness and confidence forever. Isaiah 32:17

Great peace have they who love your law, and nothing can make them stumble. Psalm 199:165

No discipline seems pleasant at the time, but painful. Later on, however, it produces a harvest of righteousness and peace for (Jan) *who* (has) *been trained by it.* Romans 12:11

Lord, you establish peace for us; all that we have accomplished you have done for us. Isaiah 26:12

"Peace I leave with you; my peace I give you. I do not give to you as the world gives. Do not let your hearts be troubled and do not be afraid." John 14:27

"I have told you these things, so that in me you may have peace. In this world you will have trouble. But take heart! I have overcome the world." John 16:33

Let the peace of Christ rule in your hearts, since as members of one body you (Jan) *were called to peace.* Colossians 3:15

Do not be anxious about anything (Jan), *but in everything by prayer and petition, with thanksgiving, present your requests to God. And the peace of God, which transcends all understanding, will guard your hearts and minds in Christ Jesus.* Philippians 4:6,7

2. COMFORT – GOD'S COMPASSION

Though he brings grief, he will show compassion, so great is his unfailing love. For he does not willingly bring affliction or grief to the children of men." Lamentations 3:32,33

The steadfast love of the Lord never ceases, his mercies never come to an end; they are new every morning; great is thy faithfulness. "The Lord is my portion," says my soul, "therefore I will hope in him." The Lord is good to those who wait for him, to the soul that seeks him. It is good that one should wait quietly for the salvation of the Lord. Lamentations 3:22-26 RSV

I am still confident of this: I will see the goodness of the Lord in the land of the living. Wait for the Lord; be strong and take heart and wait for the Lord. Psalm 27:13,14

He tends his flock like a shepherd: He gathers the lambs (you, Jan) *in his arms and carries* (you) *close to his heart; he gently leads those who have young.* Isaiah 10:11

But those who hope in the Lord will renew their strength. They will soar on wings like eagles; they will run and not grow weary, they will walk and not be faint. Isaiah 40:30,31

"You whom I took from the ends of the earth, and called from its farthest corners, saying to you, 'You are my servant, I have chosen you and not cast you off; fear not for I am with you, be not dismayed, for I am your God. I will strengthen you, I will help you, I will uphold you with my victorious right hand." Isaiah 41:9,10 RSV

"Fear not, for I have redeemed you; I have called you by name, you are mine (Jan). *When you pass through the waters I will be with you; and through the rivers, they shall not overwhelm you; and when you walk through the fire you shall not be burned, and the flame shall not consume you. For I am the Lord your God, the Holy One of Israel, your Savior...You are precious in my eyes* (Jan) *and honored and I*

love you." Isaiah 43:1-4 RSV

A bruised reed he will not break, and a smoldering wick he will not snuff out. Isaiah 42:3

3. STRENGTH

Though the fig tree does not bud and there are no grapes on the vines, though the olive crop fails and the fields produce no food, though there are no sheep in the pen and no cattle in the stalls, yet I will rejoice in the Lord, I will be joyful in God my Savior. The Sovereign Lord is my strength; he makes my feet like the feet of a deer, he enables me to go on the heights. Habakkuk 3:17-19

Hear, O Lord, and be merciful to me; O Lord, be my help. You turned my wailing into dancing; you removed my sackcloth and clothed me with joy, that my heart may sing to you and not be silent. O Lord my God, I will give you thanks forever. Psalm 31:10-12

(Jan), *God is (your) refuge and strength, an ever-present help in trouble.* Psalm 46:1

From the ends of the earth I call to you, I call as my heart grows faint; lead me to the rock that is higher than I. For you have been my refuge, a strong tower against the foe. I long to dwell in your tent forever and take refuge in the shelter of your wings. Psalm 61:2-4

My flesh and my heart may fail, but God is the strength of my heart and my portion forever. Psalm 73:26

He gives strength to the weary and increases the power of the weak. Isaiah 40:29

"My grace is sufficient for you, for my power is made perfect in weakness." 2 Corinthians 12:9

I pray that out of his glorious riches he may strengthen you with power through his Spirit in your inner being, so that Christ may dwell in your hearts through faith. Ephesians 3:16,17a

I can do all things in him who strengthens me. Philippians 4:13 RSV

4. FEAR

Have I not commanded you? Be strong and courageous. Do not be terrified; do not be discouraged, for the Lord your God will be with you wherever you go. Joshua 1:9

Even though I walk through the valley of shadow of death, I will fear no evil, for you are with me; your rod and your staff, they comfort me. Psalm 23:4

The Lord is my light and my salvation – whom shall I fear? The Lord is the stronghold of my life – of whom shall I be afraid?... For in the day of trouble he will keep me safe in the shelter of his tabernacle and set me high on a rock. Psalm 27:1,5

He will cover you (Jan) *with his feathers, and under his wings you will find refuge; his faithfulness will be your shield and rampart. You* (Jan) *will not fear the terror of night, nor the arrow that flies by day, nor the pestilence that stalks in the darkness, nor the plague that destroys at midday...If you make the Most High your dwelling – even the Lord, who is my refuge – then no harm will befall you, no disaster will come near your tent.* Psalm 91:4-5,9-10

Preserve sound judgment and discernment, do not let them out of your sight...Then you will go on your way in safety, and your foot will not stumble; when you lie down, you will not be afraid; when you lie down, your sleep will be sweet. Proverb 3:21, 23-24

For you did not receive a spirit that makes you a slave again to fear, but you received the Spirit of sonship. And by him we cry, "Abba, Father." The Spirit himself testifies with our spirit that we are God's children. Romans 8:15,16

So we know and believe the love God has for us. God is love, and he who abides in love abides in God, and God

abides in him...There is no fear in love, but perfect love casts our fear. For fear has to do with punishment, and he who fears is not perfected in love. 1 John 4:16,18 RSV

Daily Prayer for Self and the Brethren

One of the greatest gifts we can give another in the body of Christ is the offering of prayer. Below are three different Scripture references in which we can claim God's wonderful promises of hope and a future in Christ. As you read through these two sections, insert either your name or the name of a loved one in Christ wherever (name) appears. May deep contentment and assurance rest within you as you pray the Holy Spirit to carry out the beautiful promises it holds.

Ephesians 1:17-19 – *I keep asking that the God of our Lord Jesus Christ, the glorious Father, may give you* (name) *the Spirit of wisdom and revelation so that you* (name) *may know him better. I pray also that the eyes of your heart may be enlightened in order that you* (name) *may know the hope to which he has called you, the riches of his glorious inheritance in the saints, and his incomparably great power for us who believe.*

Ephesians 3:16-19 – *I pray that out of his glorious riches he may strengthen you* (name) *with power through his Spirit in your inner being* (name), *so that Christ may dwell in your hearts through faith. And I pray that you* (name), *being rooted and established in love, may have power, together with all the saints, to grasp how wide and long and high and deep is the love of Christ, and to know this love that surpasses knowledge – that you* (name) *may be filled to the measure of all the fullness of God.*

The Sword of the Spirit

Take the helmet of salvation and the sword of the Spirit,

which is the word of God. Ephesians 6:17

Nothing pierces a human soul more than the word of God. Proof of this is given in Hebrews 4:12. *For the word of God is living and active. Sharper than any double edged sword, it penetrates even to dividing soul and spirit, joints and marrow; it judges the hearts and attitudes of the heart.*

But man is not the only one stilled and stricken by God's word. Satan cringes at the proper and potent use of it. While completely learn-ed in Scripture himself, his use-out-of-context – often poisons a man's heart and soul. But when used by one in Christ, it wields as the sword of the Spirit and slashes all his attempts to disavow our firm foundation of faith.

We therefore need to learn, read and absorb Scripture promises on a regular basis. For unless we are familiar with the real, we cannot begin to detect the counterfeit. In his letter to the Hebrews, Luke reminds the readers that growth in God's word cannot exist without persistent use. But solid food (from God's word) is for the mature, who by constant use have trained themselves to distinguish good from evil. (Hebrews 5:14) As we step beyond the milk, or elementary truths of God's word, His solid food empowers and strengthens us to fight against Satan through the use of the Spirit's sword. (Hebrews 5:12)

Begin **now** to *let the word of Christ dwell in you richly as you teach and admonish one another with all wisdom, and as you sing psalms, hymns and spiritual songs with gratitude in your hearts to God.* Colossians 3:16

10. DIGGING INTO HIS WORD

An old familiar hymn resounds with power and purpose as we claim God's word in our life. As you read each verse, meditate on the complete thought it is trying to portray. Write that thought in the space provided.

1. Standing on the promises of Christ my King,
   Thru eternal ages let His praises ring;
   Glory in the highest I will shout and sing,
   Standing on the promises of God.

Refrain: Standing, standing,
   Standing on the promises of God my Savior;
   Standing, standing,
   Standing on the promises of God.

2. Standing on the promises that cannot fail,
   When the howling storms of doubt and fear assail,
   By the living word of God I shall prevail,
   Standing on the promises of God. Refrain:

3. Standing on the promises of Christ the Lord,
   Bound to Him eternally by love's strong cord,
   Overcoming daily with the Spirit's sword,
   Standing on the promises of God. Refrain:

4. Standing on the promises I cannot fall,
   List'ning ev'ry moment to the Spirit's call
   Resting in my Savior as my all in all,
   Standing on the promises of God. Refrain:

Take time during your busy schedule to read Psalm 119. The author of this Psalm displayed a deep love for God's word. He trusted God to use it to teach, strengthen, direct and preserve him. Relish the promises found therein.

Prayer: Father, Your word is truly a *lamp to my feet and a light for my path.* May Your Spirit touch my heart and spirit with an unending hunger and thirst for Your word. *Sustain me according to your promise, and I will live.* Amen (Psalm 119:105,116)

(song found in Singing Youth by Singspiration, Inc. Zondervan Publishing House, Grand Rapids, MI 49506 ©1966)

11
A Grateful Leper
Having a Thankful Heart

He walked these dusty roads before. His ministry engulfed a large area and the travel often wearied Him. But wherever the Spirit called, He went – for His Father must be glorified and His will done.

Encounters with lepers on His journeys were not uncommon. Those who had heard of the Healer, faced Him, confronted Him and begged for a release from their bodily and emotional torture. Hearing of His coming into the village, ten leprous men approached the one individual whom they believed could grant them freedom from their life of misery.

Remembering the Mosiac law in Leviticus 13:45, 46 which states, *The person with such an infectious disease must wear torn clothes, let his hair be unkempt, cover the lower part of his face and cry out, "Unclean! Unclean!" As long as he has the infection he remains unclean. He must live alone; he must live outside the camp*, they kept their distance from the Man of God. With the standard distance usually held at fifty yards, they resolved to attract His attention.

Unanimously, they cried out in persistent, loud voices, *"Jesus, Master, have pity on us!"* (Luke 17:13) Their importunity remained unabated. Their grief reflected itself in the need for pity. Resting in His compassion, they ached for His decision to be that of healing.

The Master did not step forward and touch them. He did not send them home. He did not speak a word of healing.

Rather, he spoke words of obedience. Having a deep respect and knowledge of ceremonial law, Jesus commanded the ten lepers to *"Go, show yourselves to the priests."* (Luke 17:14)

Acknowledging a wholeness of body after the uncleanness of leprosy involved ceremonial cleansing by the priest. After full examination of the priests, sacrifices needed to be made and special rituals observed. Nine of the lepers, most likely of Jewish decent, needed no further explanation. The only step facing them rested in their resolve for obedience.

Without question all ten lepers chose to return to the priests. While en route, their complete healing manifested itself. Nine men, focused on their goal, chose to continue onward to their required destination. However, one man, a Samaritan, experienced overwhelming joy and sensed a deep need to return to the Master Healer. Falling prostrate at the feet of Jesus, He praised God with exuberant voice, thanking this tender, compassionate Savior for the healing of his body.

Jesus marveled at the faith of this alien, this Samaritan. For as one who had not been privileged with the wisdom and knowledge of God as a race, he, however, revealed his faith and gratitude for the miraculous healing that had taken place. Already healed of body, Jesus turned to the Samaritan and said, *"Rise and go; your faith has made you well."* (Luke 17:19) The Samaritan, healed first in body, distinguished himself from the rest by his act of faith. His rich reward included spiritual healing.

But what of the others? Was it their resolute need to complete ceremonial law that prevented them from returning to give thanks? Desperate for a cure, where was their equal response of gratitude? Even Jesus expressed His amazement. *"Were not all ten cleansed? Where are the other nine? Was no one found to return and give praise to God except this foreigner?"* (Luke 17:17)

Poignantly revealing ingratitude, these nine men of God's

chosen race, failed to respond with grateful hearts. Returning thanks to the Giver for healing failed to enter their mind or hearts, reflecting a cure of body but a sickness of spirit. The Samaritan however found his total needs met, for both physical and spiritual healing were complete.

Where Do I Begin?

Ingratitude rests as one major problem among individuals today. While richly blessed with family, friends, material possessions, wealth, a free country, and an abundance of other gifts, the Giver of all good seldom receives His return of thanks. Just as only one of ten lepers returned to offer thanksgiving in the story, that ratio may be even greater today. Often the more numerous our blessings, the less gratitude reflected.

Observing children remains a joy of mine. Their vibrancy, their enthusiasm, their simple and unabated responses overwhelm me. Yet discouragement sometimes overpowers me when I also see their selfishness, anger and ingratitude. All too soon I realize that some of these attitudes and habits never change. These children grow up and continue in the pattern already set out in their lives. Unless submitting themselves to Christ, the same selfishness, anger and ingratitude continue to exist as adults.

I have witnessed two children in the same household, with the same parents and training, maintain such different postures in their heart. One may be loving, caring and extremely thankful and the other is centered on self. Although both know Jesus as their Savior from sin, yet old habits die a harder death in one than in another. One desires to give all he can to others, another wants all he can get. Possessing a thankful heart is resting secure in one – the other doesn't have a clue.

While most parents teach their children to say "Please"

and "Thank you" on a regular basis, I believe in my own heart that one either possesses an attitude of gratitude or he doesn't. It cannot be forced. But we as parents still need to teach this habit. Verbalizing the thankful heart, writing thank you notes and bringing thank you gifts are examples to set. Being a role model of gratitude needs to be displayed, for most in today's world have lost this precious art and privilege. If they don't learn from us, where will they learn? At least we can say, "We tried."

At the very heart of gratitude, however, rests a secure love for a Savior whose extreme price on the cross heightens our sense of gratitude. Through Him we reflect a special and sincere loving heart that gives and appreciates others. Paul reaffirms that in 2 Corinthians 2:14, *But thanks be to God, who always leads us in triumphal procession in Christ and through us spreads everywhere the fragrance of the knowledge of him.*

Through our actions, our attitude of gratitude to others, our enthusiastic expressions of appreciation, others see Him. These "gifts" become not only a sweet-smelling fragrance to others but also to God. They are a *fragrant offering, an acceptable sacrifice, pleasing to God.* (Philippians 4:18) In Him and through Him, our sacrifices of gratitude abound with His love.

Begin Now

Our Father in heaven desires thankful hearts from His loved ones. Yet many of us need lessons in gratitude. Believing the word of God to be the greatest genuine source of the growth, we can learn from those who practiced and understood the true source of a thankful heart in the past. Below are some suggested ideas for strengthening a sense of gratitude in your own heart.

Begin by making a list of abundant blessings in your life

for which to give thanks. If you have difficulty discovering those blessings, consider the following verse taken from the Amplified Bible. *Bless (affectionately, gratefully praise) the Lord, O my soul; and forget not (one of) all his benefits – Who forgives (every one of) all your iniquities. Who heals (each one of) all your diseases. Who redeems your life from the pit and corruption, Who beautifies, dignifies, and crowns you with loving-kindness and tender mercy; Who satisfies your mouth (your necessity and desire at your personal age and situation) with good so that your youth, renewed, is like the eagle's (strong, overcoming, soaring)!* (Isaiah 40:31, The Amplified Bible)

Notice these apply to the spiritual. Through Christ's redemptive sacrifice on the cross, we find forgiveness, healing of body and mind, peace in the midst of our trials and troubles, inner joy, tenderness, love, patience, gentleness, compassion, and other endless sources of strength and power. His blessings know no limits – the only limits we possess are in our own minds. All are deserving of infinite thanksgiving to the One Who made it all possible.

What God's Word Says

The one book encompassing powerful passages relating to thankfulness is the book of Psalms. This book alone, if taken to heart, can teach us beautiful lessons.

For His righteousness – *I will give thanks to the Lord because of his righteousness and will sing praise to the name of the Lord Most High.* Psalm 1:17

For being our strength and shield – *The Lord is my strength and my shield; my heart trusts in him, and I am helped. My heart leaps for joy and I will give thanks to him in song.* Psalm 28:7

For turning sorrow into joy – *Hear, O Lord, and be merciful to me; O Lord, be my help. You turned my wailing* *into dancing; you removed my sackcloth and clothed me with joy.* Psalm 30:11,12

For the nearness of His Name – *We give thanks to you, O God, we give thanks, for your Name is near; men tell of your wonderful deeds.* Psalm 75:1

For God's greatness and wondrous works – *Come, let us sing for joy to the Lord; let us shout aloud to the Rock of our salvation. Let us come before him with thanksgiving and extol him with music and song. For the Lord is the great God, the great King above all gods.* Psalm 95:1-3

For rescue from trouble – *Then they cried to the Lord in their trouble, and he saved them from their distress. He sent forth his word and healed them; he rescued them from the grave.* Psalm 107:19-20

Simply – You are my God! – *You are my God, and I will give you thanks; you are my God, and I will exalt you. Give thanks to the Lord, for he is good; His love endures forever.* Psalm 118:28,29

Psalm 100 expresses joy, worship, thanksgiving, praise and love. Commit yourself to memorizing this beautiful Psalm today. Through it may your heart be filled to overflowing with the goodness of God.

Moving Forward in Thankfulness

As we continue our search of Scripture, numerous blessings deserving of gratitude appear in the New Testament. Heroes of faith accepted and encouraged thankful hearts in others. Examples are:

For an escape from worry – *Do not be anxious about anything but in everything, by prayer and petition, with thanksgiving, present your requests to God.* Philippians 4:6

For the peace of Christ – *Let the peace of Christ rule in your hearts, since as members of one body you were called to peace. And be thankful.* Colossians 3:15

For receiving an unshakable kingdom – *Therefore, since we are receiving a kingdom that cannot be shaken, let us be thankful, and so worship God acceptably with reverence and awe, for our "God is a consuming fire."* Hebrews 12:28

For being led in triumph – *But thanks be to God, who always leads us in triumphal procession in Christ and through us spreads everywhere the fragrance of the knowledge of him.* 2 Corinthians 2:14

For allowing our service to create thankful hearts in others – *This service that you perform is not only supplying the needs of God's people but is also overflowing in many expressions of thanks to God. Because of the service by which you have proved yourselves, men will praise God for the obedience that accompanies your confession of the gospel of Christ, and for your generosity in sharing with them and with everyone else.* 2 Corinthians 9:12,13

For the abounding grace and faith of others – *I thank my God every time I remember you. In all my prayers for all of you, I always pray with joy because of your partnership in the gospel from the last day until now, being confident of this, that he who began a good work in you will carry it on to completion until the day of Christ Jesus.* Philippians 1:3-6

For the power and "equipment" to resist Satan and his army – *Therefore put on the full armor of God, so that when the day of evil comes, you may be able to stand your ground, and after you have done everything, to stand. Stand firm then, with the belt of truth buckled around your waist, with the breastplate of righteousness in place, and with your feet fitted with the readiness that comes from the gospel of peace. In addition to all this, take up the shield of faith, with which you can extinguish all the flaming arrows of the evil one. Take the helmet of salvation and the sword of the Spirit, which is the word of God.* Ephesians 6:13-17

For the mighty, redemptive work of Christ on the

cross and His example to us – *Your attitude should be the same as that of Christ Jesus: Who being in very nature God, did not consider equality with God something to be grasped, but made himself nothing, taking the very nature of a servant, being made in human likeness. And being found in appearance as a man, he humbled himself and became obedient to death – even death on a cross!* Philippians 2:5-8

Thanks be to God! What greater blessing could we receive!

Give Thanks for Difficult Circumstances?

Struggling with intense inner pain and outward circumstances, the thought of thanking God in the midst of my circumstances eluded me. Upon reading 1 Thessalonians 3:16-18, confusion presented itself. *Be joyful always; pray continually; give thanks in all circumstances for this is God's will for you in Christ Jesus.* (verses 16-18)

What did it mean to give thanks in all circumstances? I hated the circumstances I was in – why would I give thanks for them? I hated being widowed. It remained exceedingly difficult to raise four small children alone. The gut-wrenching loneliness I experienced never abated. No ounce of gratitude could be found in my soul for those painful details of my life. What was there to be thankful for?

As days rolled on into weeks, I began to realize that His goodness captured my heart. I found reason to rejoice that had nothing to do with my circumstances. I slowly began to understand that the very situations I hated turned my eyes toward Jesus. The more I desired His strength, love, and comfort, the more I began rejoicing in my circumstances. God had a divine purpose - to make me more like His Son. My circumstances didn't change for a long time but my desire to thank Him changed quickly.

The phrase in that same verse, *for this is God's will for*

you in Christ Jesus, caused me to hit another road block. How could Tom's illness and death be God's will? Did He want my children to be without a father? Was it His desire that I suffer such anguish and grief? What kind of God would allow that?

Upon studying the verse further, I slowly realized that the word *for* was referring to the first part of the verse. While the circumstances I encountered filled my life with pain and heartache, I realized that not all things (circumstances) flow from God's hand. Some are brought about by the sinful condition of the world, by Satan or perhaps by my own fleshly choices. He cannot be blamed.

While He does have the ability to stop any and all of these things from happening, He sometimes chooses not to. He does not control the world in that way. Yet He promises to be there by our side as we enter the painful walk. During that walk He says, "Be joyful always" – for this is God's will for you in Christ Jesus. "Pray continually" – for this is God's will for you in Christ Jesus. "Give thanks in all circumstances" – for this is God's will for you in Christ Jesus. The greatest test of surrender to God's divine plan for my life was thankfulness in my circumstances – for this too is God's will for you in Christ Jesus.

By the Spirit

Through the power of the Spirit, a thankful heart exudes. It manifests itself in our lives, our words and our actions. Because of the victory given to us through Christ on the cross, joy and an abundant life overpowers us. *But thanks be to God! He gives us victory through our Lord Jesus Christ.* (1 Corinthians 15:57)

There is no excuse! Employing the fruit of the Spirit, trusting in His wisdom and resting in His goodness, an attitude of gratitude develops even in trial. Absorb Him through His Word. Focus on His wondrous gift of love through the agony of the cross and the resurrection freedom. The grumps and fear will dissipate. He will be victorious!

11. Digging into His Word

But thanks be to God! He gives us the victory through our Lord Jesus Christ. Romans 7:25

At the height of Tom's illness, fatigue and frustration overwhelmed me. Sensing my vulnerability, Satan sought opportunity to derail me. As I wept in despair one evening, I heard a voice say, "Give up on God." Somewhat stunned, I listened quietly. Again I heard the words, "Give up on God." Realizing the consequences of such a decision, I became angry – not at God but at the absurd suggestion. With fists clinched and jaw tightened, I spoke loudly, "No, I will not give up on God. Satan, get out of here, for I have victory in Jesus Christ and you cannot take that away from me." With that the weeping ceased and peace flooded my spirit.

Realizing what had just taken place, exclamations of gratitude flowed from my lips. The greatest blessing of my life had been realized – the victory over Satan through Christ the crucified.

Take time to read and meditate over the next five Bible references. Pray that the Spirit enable you to fully comprehend the power and grace available through Christ and the cross. At the end, write a prayer of thanksgiving for His extreme sacrifice made on your behalf.

Romans 5:1-5

Ephesians 3:16-21

Colossians 1:15-20

Hebrews 12:1-3

1 John 4:9-10

Jan Brunette

For it is by grace you have been saved, through faith – and this not from yourselves, it is the gift of God – not by works so that no one can boast. Ephesians 2:8-9

Prayer: (to be written by you)

12
THE PRAISE OF A KING
God Deserves Praise

The joyous celebration swallowed up the anger and fear that had existed months earlier. The awesome acceptance of God's presence replaced the horrors of Uzzah's death. The carefully planned moving of the ark by the Levites softened the terror of incorrectly transporting the ark of the covenant three months earlier.

King David's failure to study the Mosaic laws endangered the lives of those who chose to transport the ark with an oxen-drawn cart. Forgetting that God's untouchable presence sat enthroned between the cherubim of the ark (1 Samuel 4:4), David failed to heed the warning in Numbers 4:15. *After Aaron and his sons have finished covering the holy furnishings and all the holy articles, and when the camp is ready to move, the Kohathites* (branch of the Levites) *are to come to do the carrying. But they must not touch the holy things or they will die. The Kohathites are to carry those things that are in the Tent of Meeting.* (parenthesis mine)

The oxen-drawn cart, hardly appropriate for the bearing of the Almighty God, needed to be laid upon the shoulders of God's own chosen priests. Defined clearly to Moses, God's instructions were clear. *"Have them make a chest of acacia wood – two and a half cubits long, a cubit and a half wide, and a cubit and a half high. Overlay it with pure gold, both inside and out, and make a gold molding around it. Cast four gold rings for it and fasten them to its four feet, with two rings on one side and two rings on the other. Then make poles of acacia wood and overlay them with gold. Insert the poles into the rings on the sides of the chest to carry it. The poles are to remain in the rings of this ark; they are not be removed."* (Exodus 25:10-16)

After reading this, David more fully understand the error of his previous transportation of the ark. No mistakes would be made this time. He announced to the people, *"No one but the Levites may carry the ark of God, because the Lord chose them to carry the ark of the Lord and to minister before him forever."...And the Levites carried the ark of God with the poles on their shoulders, as Moses had commanded in accordance with the word of the Lord.* (1 Chronicles 15:2,15) Ecstatically David beheld the mighty ark of the covenant as it moved ever so slowly toward its tent home prepared for it in the City of David. With a rejoicing spirit, David offered sacrifices of a bull and a fattened calf after every six paces. Trumpets moved before the ark of God and doorkeepers for the ark were assigned. *David told the leaders of the Levites to appoint their brothers as singers to sing joyful songs, accompanied by musical instruments; lyres, harps and cymbals.* (1 Chronicles 15:16)

David's praise to God could not be contained. Entering the City of David, his heart filled to overflowing. Putting on a linen robe and wearing an ephod (priestly vest), he leaped and danced before the Lord. As singers sang, instruments played, trumpets blew and the entire people of Israel shouted, David became fully aware of the Name, the name of the Lord Almighty. His intense joy manifested itself as he danced before the Lord with all his might. (2 Samuel 6:2,14)

Now in its home, the tent prepared for housing the presence of God, *David sacrificed burnt offerings and fellowship offerings before the Lord. After he had finished sacrificing the burnt offerings and fellowship offerings, he blessed the people in the name of the Lord Almighty. Then he gave a loaf of bread, a cake of dates and a cake of raisins to each person*

in the whole crowd of Israelites, both men and women.
(2 Samuel 6:17,19)

David's spirit overflowed even more as he presented a thanksgiving psalm to Asaph, the chief musician to be sung on this festive occasion. Set to music, the words of praise and honor flowed. *"Sing to the Lord, all the earth; proclaim his salvation day after day. Declare his glory among the nations, his marvelous deeds among all peoples. For great is the Lord and most worthy of praise; he is to be feared above all gods. For all the gods of the nations are idols, but the Lord made the heavens. Splendor and majesty are before him; strength and joy in his dwelling place. Ascribe to the Lord, O families of nations, ascribe to the Lord glory and strength, ascribe to the Lord the glory due his name. Bring an offering and come before him; worship the Lord in the splendor of his holiness. Tremble before him, all the earth! The world is firmly established; it cannot be moved. Let the heavens rejoice, let the earth be glad; let them say among the nations, 'The Lord reigns!' Let the sea resound, and all that is in it; let the fields be jubilant, and everything in them! Then the trees of the forest will sing, they will sing for joy before the Lord, for he comes to judge the earth. Give thanks to the Lord, for he is good; his love endures forever...Praise to the Lord, the God of Israel, from everlasting to everlasting."* (1 Chronicles 16:23-34,36)

Then all the people said "Amen" and "Praise the Lord." (1 Chronicles 16:36b) *And all the people went to their homes.* (2 Samuel 6:19b) *To complete the work, David left Asaph and his associates before the ark of the covenant of the Lord to minister there regularly, according to each day's requirements.* (1 Chronicles 16:36b, 37)

Excitedly David returned home to bless his own household. But unfortunately, admonishment and belittlement greeted him. His wife Michal, who watched his excitement, his disrobing of his kingly garments, his embarrassing dance in the streets, met him with harsh words. *"How the king of Israel has distinguished himself today, disrobing in the sight of the slave of his servants as any vulgar fellow would!"* (2 Samuel 6:20)

Refusing to allow her loathsome attitude to dampen his spirits, he acknowledges his willingness to belittle himself by stripping himself of his kingly robes, replacing them with priestly robes. *"It was before the Lord, who chose me rather than your father or anyone from his house when he appointed me ruler over the Lord's people Israel – I will celebrate before the Lord. I will become even more undignified than this, and I will be humiliated in my own eyes. But by these slave girls you spoke of, I will be held in honor."* (2 Samuel 6:21,22)

His God was worthy of praise, even at the cost of his own dignity. His own conscience cleared him of wrongdoing. With his goal that of God's glorification, opinions and attitudes of others mattered not. Man's reproach could not dampen his joy.

God holiness, His majesty, His splendor, His strength, His mighty power, now dwelt in the holy place, between the cherubim on the throne – in the tent prepared for Him. The return of the ark to the holy city and the God who sat upon the throne, deserved praise, reverence and awe. God not only remained on His earthly throne. He also dwelt in the heart of a king.

Praise Versus Problems

As the deer pants for streams of water, so my soul pants for you, O God. My soul thirsts for God, for the living God. When can I go and meet with God.?...Why are you downcast, O my soul? Why so disturbed within me? Put your hope in God, for I will yet praise him, my Savior and my God. (Psalm 42:1,2,5)

Shuddering and shaking, sweat covered my entire body. Fear engulfed me night after night, causing sleeplessness, and smothering me while at work. Relief seemed far from sight. But the Spirit's goodness remained. His presence did not leave.

A friend recommended a book entitled *Healing for Damaged Emotions* by David Seamonds. As the Spirit led me through the book, one thought refreshed me. "Jan, praise God! Think of anything and everything you can for which to praise God."

Remembering that a person's mind can only think one thought at a time, I resolutely dug in my heals in an attempt to dispel fear. If my mind praised God, I could not dwell on fear. Even as the night sweats and the burning sensation in my neck and shoulders persisted, I continued to constantly and rapidly praise God – sometimes only repeating the words "Praise you, Jesus. Praise you, Father". I knew deep in my heart that He was worthy of additional praise yet my spirit was incapable of saying more at the time.

I discovered my sleep gradually increased from two to four hours, then to six. I especially enjoyed praising God for the birds at 5:00 a.m., as their melodious songs declared the break of morning. My sleepless nights were slowly being replaced with quiet slumber through God's loving response to praise.

As I filled my mind with praise at home, at school and in the evening, my determination to break the cycle of fear dominated my life. Several years passed before it subsided, yet the depth of God's love revealed through that fear overwhelmed me. I soon realized that it was fear that motivated me to seek God's face and to desire more of Him in my life.

Many nights in my search for Him, I experienced a warmth and peace beyond description. Often feeling wrapped in His everlasting arms, I imagined myself covered by the pinions of His wings. A sense of hiding within His tender heart comforted me. I began to relish my special times with Him and ached for His presence often. Praise became a vital part of my life and joy emerged in the midst of my darkest hours. How awesome, loving and compassionate my God proved to be. Praise chased the shades of darkness away and released me to trust Him more!

Praise Versus Satan's Deceptions

Satan's greatest playground takes shelter in our minds. His lies, his deceptions, his manipulations find a haven in far too many. Often assuming we are at fault for the evil thoughts that enter the recesses of our mind – guilt, fear, lust, desire for the material, etc. – we struggle with shame. Praise can release Satan's hold on our mind. It chases him away and allows God to fill that wonderful space in our brain. Delving into God's word and claiming His goodness through the promises of Scripture must follow. Desiring the mind of Christ, praying for the indwelling presence of the Spirit and holding tightly to our communication to Him through prayer and His word need ever be present. Never fail to claim Christ's victory won over Satan on the cross. Remember – the battle is already completed. The victory is ours.

If words fail to surface because of our own inadequacies, reading a Psalm of praise can replace our own words. For example, as we learned in a previous chapter, read portions of Psalm 145 as follows: *I will exalt you, my God the King; I will praise your name for ever and ever. Every day I will praise you and extol your name for ever and ever. Great (are you) Lord and most worthy of praise. (Your) greatness no one can fathom...(you) Lord (are) gracious and compassionate, slow to anger and rich in love. (You) Lord (are) good to (me; you have) compassion on all (you have) made.* (words in parenthesis indicate changes in pronouns and verbs, verses 1-3,8-9)

Praise God daily and often for Who He is and His mighty acts. Praise Jesus for His sacrificial redemption on the cross. Never forget the price He paid for your freedom – of mind, body and spirit. Thank Him also for being there for you in the midst of the valley of darkness. Grow in Him – better yet – grow in love with Him!

Peter in his letter to the scattered Christians in exile writes, *Be self-controlled and alert. Your enemy the devil prowls around like a roaring lion, looking for someone to devour. Resist him, standing firm in the faith, because you know that your brothers throughout the world are undergoing the same kind of sufferings. And the God of all grace, who called you to his eternal glory in Christ, after you have suffered a little while, will himself restore you and make you strong, firm and steadfast. To him be the power for ever and ever. Amen.* By a deliberate act of mind we need to resist the devil – and in so doing he must flee. Praise God for His goodness in being there for us in the midst of our suffering and during our struggles of the mind with Satan. (I Peter 5:8-11)

Remember the king who worshiped God with joyous abandonment. As the joy in his spirit overwhelmed and motivated him to react in total freedom, release yourself to praise. As the Spirit leads, praise Him in your circumstances and through them – in your bedroom, during your devotions, and in other locations in which you feel comfortable. But never fail to praise Him – for He is worthy of praise!

Praise the Lord, all you nations; extol him, all you peoples. For great is his love toward us, and the faithfulness of the Lord endures forever. Praise the Lord. (Psalm 117)

David A. Seamands, Healing for Damaged Emotions Workbook (Wheaton, IL: Victor Books, 1992) p.175

12. DIGGING INTO HIS WORD

My heart and soul absorbed the beautiful music and dynamic speakers. Many times, especially during the glorious songs, I desired to lift hands in praise. But being raised in a church where order in worship exists, I refrained. Instead I closed my eyes and rested in the thought of the awesome God I had grown to love.

Later, as I read the story of David, I visualized the reality of David's praise through dance. His intense joy in God's presence could not be restrained. By the same token, I understood my desire to raise holy hands yet acknowledged that my fear of embarrassment and my upbringing restricted the ability to react.

David's relationship with the Lord possessed few inhibitions. Understanding God's worthiness, he chose to use his lips, his hands, his feet and his musical instruments in praise. To enlighten and refresh you in this area, I encourage you to look up the following passages, many written by David.

They consist of two sets of verses. The first set refers to God's worthiness. The second set exposes David's need to offer praise.

Set I

Deuteronomy 7:21

Deuteronomy 10:17,21

Psalm 18:3

Psalm 47 (entire chapter)

Psalm 48:1,10,14

Psalm 62:5-8

Psalm 77:13-14

Psalm 100:3

Philippians 2:5-11

Set II

Psalm 57:7-8

Psalm 63:3-4

Psalm 69:30

Psalm 134:2

Psalm 141:2

Psalm 147:1,7

Psalm 149:3-6a

Colossians 3:16-17

1Timothy 2:8

Now make a list of ways you are willing to praise. Conclude by telling God why you believe He is worthy of your praise.
Prayer: Read Psalm 150.

13
A HIGH PRIESTLY EXAMPLE
Bringing Glory to the Father

Before Him looms the greatest test of love known to man, yet He would not allow Himself to falter. In words earlier spoken, He said, *"Now my heart is troubled, and what shall I say? 'Father, save me from this hour'? No, it was for this very reason I came to this hour. Father, glorify your name!"* (John 12:27,28a) Knowing that His body and spirit would be lanced with excruciating agony, He realizes that His earthly ministry nears completion.

His oneness with the Father creates a need to communicate. Reflecting His ultimate desire to glorify the Father, a prayer of dedication begins. Using this prayer as His High Priestly prayer, Jesus chooses to honor the Father by obedience. *"I have brought you glory on earth by completing the work you gave me to do."* (John 17:4) Through that glorification He Himself will be rewarded with a return to the previous glories of heaven, a richness He forfeited in His humanity. But His desire didn't end there.

Knowing the mission and ministries of His chosen still lay ahead, He prays for the future glory of His own disciples and their followers for all time to come. Many bless-ed were called by God out of this world and given to Jesus to serve and to love. *"I have revealed you to those whom you gave me out of the world. They were yours; you gave them to me and they have obeyed your word...For I gave them the words you gave me and they accepted them. They knew with certainty that I came from you, and they believed that you sent me...All*

I have is yours, and all you have is mine. And glory has come to me through them." (John 17:6,8,10)

Realizing His departure is near, Jesus desires divine protection for His disciples from the Father in His absence. He understands all too well the dangers and temptations they will soon face. *"I will remain in the world not longer, but they are still in the world, and I am coming to you. Holy Father, protect them by the power of your name – the name you gave me – so that they may be one as we are one...My prayer is not that you take them out of the world but that you protect them from the evil one ... Sanctify them by the truth; your word is truth."* (John 17:11,15,17) Knowing their mission on earth to be far from complete, He does not ask the Father to remove them from the world – but hold them for safe-keeping until their ministry is complete.

A primary interest of the Master also rests in the individuals who will soon follow in the train of these saintly disciples. *"My prayer is not for them alone. I pray also for those who will believe in me through their message."* (John 17:20) His eyes focused toward eternity, Jesus prays for the future generations of saints. His desire for them is oneness, glory and complete unity.

His prayer nearly complete, He focuses on all His chosen and the eternal pleasures of glory – His glory. No greater gift can be given to them than to wear the crown of glory bought with the price of a crown of thorns.

"Father, I want those you have given me to be with me where I am, and to see my glory, the glory you have given me because you loved me before the creation of the world. Righteous, Father, though the world does not know you, I know you, and they know that you have sent me. I have made you known to them, and will continue to make you known in order that the love you have for me may be in them and that I myself may be in them." (John 17:24-26)

Created for His Glory

"You are my witnesses," declares the Lord, "and my servant whom I have chosen so that you may know and believe me and understand that I am he. Before me no god was formed, nor will there be one after me. I, even I, am the Lord, and apart from me there is no savior. I have revealed and saved and proclaimed – I, and not some foreign god among you. You are my witnesses," declares the Lord, "that I am God." (Isaiah 43:10-12)

I am no mistake! Isn't that exciting? Not only is that fact true but nothing and no one has touched my life without God's overseeing eye. That fact is extremely difficult for many to swallow. Low self-esteem runs rampant. Painful, devastating torments occur in our past. Evil people invade our privacy and injure us physically, mentally and spiritually. Loss of loved ones invade our comfort zone, death destroys the family unit, rebellious children create unrelenting heartache. Yet God promises to work it out for our good and His glory. (Romans 8:28) How is that possible? Why didn't this all-seeing God stop it before the evil happened?

I personally cannot answer that question. But I do believe that God grieves with us in our circumstances *for God does not willingly bring affliction or grief to the children of men.* (Lamentations 3:33) Upon Tom's burial, the sun shone brightly. Yet at the end of the committal service, one cloud appear and a light rain shower occurred. Noticing the event, I remarked to a friend, "See, even the Lord is crying with me over Tom's death." Just as Jesus wept when Lazarus died and as He cried over Jerusalem, so I believes He cries and mourns with us.

I also experience times in my life in which He occasionally burdens me with intense grief for situations and individuals that I cannot explain – especially if they are related to children and women. This grief may occur for days and is always coupled with intense prayers. I believe that again, He is grieving through me. I am His vessel and His grief motivates me to pray.

Did you know He even keeps a record of **your** tears? *Thou hast kept count of my tossings; put thou my tears in thy bottle! Are they not in thy book?* (Psalm 56:8 RSV) His heart must ache beyond comprehension when His children are abused or mistreated or stricken in any way. But being a God who desires eternal good, often the pain must persist.

Job was a classic example. Satan attacked him with a vengeance and Job knew not why. But the source of comfort through this dynamic Old Testament book is God's power in action – power over Satan. Satan was allowed to inflict Job – but only within limits. God knew the strength of Job's faith, coupled with His Spirit's power, to resist the temptation to give up. God held Satan on a leash. In the same way **nothing** is going to touch your life that He doesn't hold the leash and offer the power. He promises a way of escape in temptation. He promises to grant you His strength. He promises to turn the suffering for your good.

Through it all God asks, "What are you going to do with it?" Will you become angry and blame it all on God or will you yield it to Him and pray for a ministry where your experience can help to further His kingdom? *Praise be to the God and Father of our Lord Jesus Christ, the Father of compassion and the God of all comfort, who comforts us in all our troubles, so that we can comfort those in any trouble with the comfort we ourselves have received from God. For just as the sufferings of Christ flow over into our lives, so also through Christ our comfort overflows.* (2 Corinthians 1:3-5)

Will you become bitter, rejecting the cleansing of spirit that God offers, or will you rejoice in His forgiveness and become an ambassador for Christ? *We are therefore Christ's ambassadors, as though God were making his appeal through us. We implore you on Christ's behalf: Be reconciled to God. God made him who had no sin to be sin for us, so that in him we might become the righteousness of God.* (2 Corinthians 5:20,21) Remember, it's not what happens to you that counts, but how you react to what happens.

As chosen children of God, we have exciting ministries – all include communication with Him through prayer and all are aimed at the glory of God. Are you up to the task?

I sometimes like to refer to myself as an alien – for I came from another kingdom, God's kingdom, to do God's work. No matter what my circumstances of life, that does not change. Only through constant connection with the source of power and strength, the true Vine, can I carry out that ministry effectively even if includes heartache, pain and anguish. (See John 15)

The result – joy! *"I have told you this so that my joy may be in you and that your joy may be complete."* (John 15:11) *"Until now you have not asked for anything in my name. Ask and you will receive, and your joy will be complete."* (John 16:24) *You have made known to me the path of life; you will fill me with joy in your presence, with eternal pleasures at your right hand.* (Psalm 16:11) *Truly He will bring me to his holy mountain and give me joy in His house of prayer.* (Isaiah 56:7)

In My Life

To you, O Lord, I called; to the Lord I cried for mercy: "What gain is there in my destruction, in my going down into the pit? Will the dust praise you? Will it proclaim your faithfulness? Hear, O Lord, and be merciful to me; O Lord, be my help" You turned my wailing into dancing; you removed my sackcloth and clothed me with joy, that my heart may sing to you and not be silent. O Lord my God, I will give you thanks forever. (Psalm 30:10-12)

Where do I find myself today? How has God used me? Has His glory been revealed through my events of the past? All I can say is "Wow! Where do I begin?"

Through the constant witness of His Spirit, my spiritual life leaped beyond all human comprehension. A hunger and thirst for the word evolved. In my heart, an eternal ache for His presence and His will came to the forefront. At times I so strongly desired to do His will, in spite of my humanness, that tears flowed. Prayer becomes continuous – a stream of living waters. Whether driving in a car, sewing, or cooking, my thoughts traveled to Him. Prayer came to the forefront in my relationship with Him – how could love and life with Him exist otherwise?

I relished in His precious times during the night when His inner peace overwhelmed me. Surrendering all to Him became easier for I realized that only in Him would the problems become lighter.

Worry, although often a temptation, became less frequent. Realizing that worry consists of two areas: a need for my own control over a situation and a lack of trust in His loving control – I find it easier to cast it all on Him. I also accepted the fact that Satan himself loves to see me get worked up over a situation and that alone makes me angry enough to rest it at Jesus' feet. I refuse to let Satan win.

The following verses have tremendous impact during these times. *Humble yourselves, therefore, under God's mighty hand, that he may lift you up in due time. Cast all your anxiety on him because he cares for you. Be self-controlled and alert. Your enemy the devil prowls around like a roaring lion looking for someone to devour. Resist him, standing firm in the faith, because you know that your brothers throughout the world are undergoing the same kind of sufferings. And the God of all grace, who called you to his eternal glory in Christ, after you have suffered a little while,*

will himself restore you and make you strong, firm and steadfast. To him be the power for ever and ever. Amen.
1 Peter 5:6-11

My ministries have broadened. Often I am amazed at the potential granted me through His Spirit. No end seems to be in sight and I wouldn't want it any other way. I become excited whenever I think of the power, love and self-control to be claimed. It is not naturally mine – believe me, I am all to weak and fallible. But through His Spirit, He knows no limits. All He needs is my willing heart and trusting spirit.

His glory manifested itself also in my role as wife and mother. Greater vistas opened after marrying again. I am currently blessed with four children of my own, seven stepchildren and twenty-two grandchildren. In the family as a whole, God nourished us with committed, dedicated Christians who serve the Lord in varied and dynamic areas. All live as examples of His abiding goodness. Although it did not come without a price, His gentle reminders of love and support have always been there.

In life, in service, in trials, in prayer, God's answer remained the same. Through the blood of Christ shed on Calvary, all my mistakes, foibles, inadequacies are erased. In Him rests all that I need. And this is my prayer: *that your love may abound more and more in knowledge and depth of insight, so that you may be able to discern what is best and may be pure and blameless until the day of Christ, filled with the fruit of righteousness that comes through Jesus Christ – to the glory and praise of God.* (Philippians 1:9-11)

13. Digging into His Word

Splendor and majesty are before him; strength and joy in his dwelling place. Ascribe to the Lord, O families of nations, ascribe to the Lord glory and strength, ascribe to the Lord the glory due his name. Bring an offering and come before him; worship the Lord in the splendor of his holiness.
(1 Chronicles 16:27-29)

Dictionary definitions for the word "glory" are numerous. All are appropriate. Examples are:
1. Exalted honor, praise, or distinction accorded by common consent
2. Something that brings honor or renown
3. A highly praiseworthy asset
4. Adoration, praise and thanksgiving offered in worship
5. Majestic beauty and splendor
6. The splendor and bliss of heaven; a state of perfect happiness. (1)

At the height of heavenly ecstasy, David displayed awesome respect for God. Recognizing the power of His Name, David cried out for others to *"ascribe to the Lord the glory due his name."* The same love David revealed for the Almighty God manifested itself in others as well.

Study the following verses which acknowledge the glory of God – the glory due His name. Record the one(s) who declare that glory.

Exodus 15:11

Exodus 33:17-23

1 Chronicles 29:10-13

Psalm 19:1

Psalm 29:1-9

Isaiah 6:1-3

Isaiah 66:18

Luke 2:14

Romans 4:18-22

Romans 11:33-36

Romans 16:25-27

Philippians 2:10-11

2 Peter 1:17

Revelation 19:1,2a

Jan Brunette

Wallowing in the presence of God we not only see His glory but chose to reflect it; that is, His honor, His adoration, His majestic beauty and splendor.

Prayer: *For I resolved to know nothing while I was with you except Jesus Christ and him crucified...so that your faith might not rest on men's wisdom but on God's power. To God be the glory. Amen* (1 Corinthians 2:2,5)

(1) Joseph H. Friend and David B. Guralnik, eds, Webster's New World Dictionary, College Edition (Cleveland and New York, 1960), p.616

14
AT HIS FEET
Listen and Grow in His Word

SCENE 1

In an obscure village, two miles from Jerusalem, He found a haven. Bethany lacked the hustle and bustle of Jerusalem yet housed the love and fellowship of friends. Often Jesus desired to rest in this little town as it offered Him the solitude He craved.

Jesus and his disciples chose the home of Martha, Mary and Lazarus as a rest stop on this particular journey into Jerusalem. As was typical of her, Martha busied herself in the kitchen, preparing a complete, meticulous meal for her honored guest. Desiring to go all out, she fretted and stewed over the menu, the decorations, and the preparations. After all, this was Jesus – the promised Messiah. How could she do any other than spend a great deal of time fulfilling her need to have it be the best meal ever!

She became irritated that Mary ignored her sister's busyness. Her stirring about and her huffing at times seemed to go unnoticed by Mary – she obviously didn't care about all the work her sister had to do. Didn't Jesus notice that Mary wasn't helping? Couldn't He do something to intervene?

"Lord, don't you care that my sister has left me to do the work by myself? Tell her to help me," Martha asked. (Luke 10:40)

Noticing the error of her thinking, the irritation, the cumbersome flurry of activity, Jesus desired that she spend less time preparing an elaborate meal and spend more time in fellowship with her guest. His need of intimacy, of rest, of opening His word to those He loved, emanated as His precious goal. Yet Martha, too concerned with all her labors, had failed to understand. Observing Mary sitting at His feet, absorbing His every word, created in Him an overwhelming appreciation of her powerful need to be close to Him. How He desired that for Martha as well!

"Martha, Martha," the Lord answered, "you are worried and upset about many things, but only one thing is needed. Mary has chosen what is better, and it will not be taken away from her." (Luke 10:41,42)

Observing Jesus' need for companionship and her own need to be with Christ and receive His word, Mary's motivation rested in that reality. Because of this she was honored by the one who bestows true honor and received praise from Him for being a zealous disciple.

SCENE 2

Weeks later, the scenario at Mary and Martha changes to intense grief and sorrow. Having been ill for days, their beloved brother Lazarus succumbed to death. Jesus, who knew of His illness and impending death, refrained from entering Bethany immediately for in His spirit, He knew God's glory would be revealed in a magnificent manner. Yet while nearing their house, He is met by Martha who in anguish creates a need to admonish Him for His late return. *"Lord, if you had been here, my brother would not have died. But I know that even now God will give you whatever you ask."* (John 11:21,22)

Acknowledging her acceptance of Jesus as the Resurrection and the Life, Martha clings to the hope that Jesus will somehow restore Lazarus – in this life or the hereafter. While being a natural dynamo of activity often took her spiritual resolve away from the need to sit at Jesus' feet, she maintains a true and saving faith. Her eyes could look up to the Master and rest in His choices, for herself and for Lazarus.

Being informed of His return, Mary, with burdened heart, races toward the Friend who loved them all. Having experienced His love many times, she again falls at His feet, wailing and hysterically shrieking over her brother's death. Her concern echoes that of her sister's – *"Lord, if you had been here, my brother would not have died."* (John 11:32) In the midst of her grief, she too is consumed with a heart that questions His choice of timing.

Overwhelmed with the sight of this dearly loved sister sobbing at His feet, Jesus encounters complete compassion. Displaying intense love for her and for those Jews weeping around her, groans exude from His body. Trembling, His heart is wrung with anguish. The loss of another through death, absorbs Him as no other. His expression of love through sympathy, takes command. Succumbing to the grief, He reflects His true manhood – as He weeps with those who weep.

After the weeping subsides Jesus, deeply moved again, moves toward the tomb of Lazarus. Although in the grave for several days, He asks Martha to have the stone removed. Concerned about the smell of the decaying body, Martha is reluctant to follow His instructions yet Jesus encourages her with the words, *"Did I not tell you that if you believed, you would see the glory of God."* (John 11:40)

As the attending Jews roll the stone away, Jesus lifts His eyes to heaven and says, *"Father, I thank you that you have heard me. I knew that you always hear me, but I said this for the benefit of the people standing here, that they may believe that you sent me."* When he had said this, Jesus called in a loud voice. "Lazarus, come out!" (John 11:41,42)

Those present stand in awe as the former dead man walks out of the grave, wrapped in the strips of linen, the burial cloth still on His face. Jesus instructs them to *"Take off the grave clothes and let him go."* (John 11:44)

The sincere faith of Mary, who had again rested all at His feet, witnessed a revelation of God's glory in a sensational manner.

SCENE 3

A celebration seemed in order. Jesus came to visit again and needed to be honored for His outstanding miracle. In her usual manner, Martha served the meal while her brother reclined at the table with Jesus. Laughs were shared and love revealed. The meal only finalized the joy of the occasion.

Without advance notice, Mary demonstrates her love once more for the Messiah, the Anointed One. Having in her possession a bottle of very expensive perfume, called nard, she proceeds to pour the perfume over Jesus' feet. Reflecting devotion to the one who allowed her to sit at His feet, she chose to perform an act of servitude by washing His feet – not just with water, but at a costly price to her. Not only this act of service, but a demonstration of humility proceeded from her, as she used her hair (something to remain covered by Jewish women) to dry His feet. An act of total surrender erased all thoughts of the shame which could be brought upon her by such an act.

Those feet represented sacrifice, not only for her but, in the future, from Him. While reprimanded by others for her expensive waste, Jesus announced that her sacrifice would indeed be the burial perfume used upon His soon-to-be nailed-pierced feet .

Mary's love and devotion reflected itself in the ability and desire to remain at Jesus' feet. As she washed and dried them, the room filled with fragrance of her love-gift. She became the aroma of Christ to those present and the sweet-smelling memory of sacrificial, dedicated love to those who read of her in the future. (John 12:1-8)

Abide in His Word – Sit at His Feet

"If you remain in me and my words remain in you, ask whatever you wish, and it will be given you." (John 15:7)

Falling in love with God's word warms me more than any other blessing granted through difficulty. Discovering Christ, tasting of His goodness, being refreshed by His Spirit – all granted through constant use of His word fill my life daily. Many verses are repeated often. Some are memorized, with a goal of many more to be brought to memory. Desiring Christ's presence motivates me as I search the Scriptures. I can deeply relate to the words of Paul given to Timothy to *continue in what you have learned and have become convinced of, because you know those from whom you learned it, and how from infancy you have known the holy Scriptures, which are able to make you wise for salvation through faith in Christ Jesus. All Scripture is God-breathed and is useful for teaching, rebuking, correcting and training in righteousness, so that the man of God may be thoroughly equipped for every good work.* (2 Timothy 3:14-17)

As with any other accomplishment in life, fulfillment means commitment, dedication and time spent in search and research. Being a Bible teacher for many years, I realize all too well that the one who teaches learns more than the one being taught. I never regret that emphasis in my life. As time passes, still today, my hunger and thirst for Biblical knowledge is insatiable. How I praise God for that blessing!

To sit at His feet requires time spent there, just as with Mary. All too often hectic schedules, family commitments and seemingly endless responsibilities prevent many from coming into His presence. But Jesus cries out to all as He did to Martha, *"You are worried and upset about many things, but only one thing is needed. Mary has chosen what is better, and it will not be taken away from her."* (Luke 10:41,42) He also promises that if we place Him first in life, our other needs will be filled. *"But seek first his kingdom and his righteousness and all these things will be given to you as well. Therefore do not worry about tomorrow, for tomorrow will worry about itself. Each day has enough trouble of its own."* (Matthew 6:33,34)

The longest chapter in the Psalms expresses more eloquently the wonder and pleasure of God's word. *"Oh, how I love your law! I meditate on it all day long. Your commands make me wiser than my enemies, for they are ever with me...How sweet are your words to my taste, sweeter than honey to my mouth! I gain understanding from your precepts; therefore I hate every wrong path. Thy word is a lamp to my feet and a light for my path...Your statutes are my heritage forever; they are the joy of my heart. My heart is set on keeping your decrees to the very end.* (Psalm 119:97-98,101-105, 111-112)

I earnestly believe that through communication with Christ in His word, we radiate His very presence. What greater privilege than to shine as stars for Him, to radiate His love to others, to be the fragrance of life to the body of Christ!

Those who look to him are radiant; their faces are never covered with shame. (Psalm 34:5)

Rest in Him – Wait!

Vacations usually re-energize me. Taking time to rest, to relax, and to be away from ringing phones and commitments create calmness. Even my brain functions better upon return as the pace and level of stress decreases. How I thank God for those precious times away from the routines at home.

Times of rest, vacations, are also needed in my spiritual life. When events occur that seem endless, when the stress level is at a peak for months, when my spirit is in turmoil, God desires that I rest in Him. *Find rest, O my soul, in God alone; my hope comes from him. He alone is my rock and my salvation; he is my fortress, I will not be shaken. My salvation and my honor depend on God; he is my mighty rock, my refuge. Trust in him at all times, O people; pour out your hearts to him, for God is our refuge.* (Psalm 62:5-8) *He who dwells in the shelter of the Most High will rest in the shadow of the Almighty. I will say of the Lord, "He is my refuge and my fortress, my God, in whom I trust."...He will cover you with his feathers, and under his wings you will find refuge; his faithfulness will be your shield and rampart.* (Psalm 91:1-2,4)

Resting in His presence creates peace and calmness. With concentration on His promises to be my refuge, my salvation, my mighty rock, my fortress, the focus turns from self to Him. As I fix my eyes on Jesus and set my mind and heart on heavenly things, He flips my inner world upside down. While outward circumstances may not change, the spirit within me becomes at rest. Closing my eyes to the world, its trials and tribulations, I become revitalized. The sense of being covered by His feathers and hidden under His wings floods over me as feelings of protection and safety become apparent.

Often resting involves a period of waiting – a task most difficult in this world of instant gratification and quick fixes. Yet it is in the waiting and resting that His eternal purpose bubbles forth. The greatest degree of growth takes place during these times. King David discovered that all too well.

We wait in hope for the Lord; he is our help and our shield. In him our hearts rejoice, for we trust in his holy name. May your unfailing love rest upon us, O Lord, even as we put our hope in you. (Psalm 33:20-22)

I am still confident of this: I will see the goodness of the Lord in the land of the living. Wait for the Lord; be strong and take heart and wait for the Lord. (Psalm 27:13,14)

I waited patiently for the Lord; he turned to me and heard my cry. He lifted me out of the slimy pit, out of the mud and mire; he set my feet on a rock and gave me a firm place to stand. He put a new song in my mouth, a hymn of praise to our God. Many will see and fear and put their trust in the Lord. (Psalm 40:1-3)

My favorite verse, found in Isaiah, contains a wonderful promise for those who wait. *But they who wait for the Lord shall renew their strength, they shall mount up with wings like eagles, they shall run and not be weary, they shall walk and not faint.* (Isaiah 40:31) What a joy it is to soar with the eagles!

Quiet Times Alone – Listen

Part of resting and waiting is the lost art of being quiet. Listening to music helps so much when trying to focus on His kingdom. I deeply understand why King Saul found soothing refreshment in the sound of David's harp. Quiet, calm music – music with spiritual words that can be understood – serve to quiet the spirit. It brings me to a place where I can hide. As I say, *"You are my hiding place; you will protect me from trouble and surround me with songs of deliverance,"* the Lord responds, *"I will instruct you and teach you in the way you should go: I will counsel you and watch over you."* (Psalm 32:7,8)

Meditating on a particular verse comforts my soul. One I love to think about often is Zephaniah 3:17. *The Lord your God is with you, he is mighty to save. He will take great delight in you, he will quiet you with his love, he will rejoice over you with singing.* What a tremendous verse to establish and nourish my self-esteem! He delights in me – just as I am. As I remain quiet before Him, He quiets me. The best part – He actually rejoices over me with singing. I often try picture Him and His angels singing over me. The thought is deeply moving to me.

Offering praise during quiet times touches His soul and refreshes mine. If my words of praise are difficult, I often use the words of David. His final recorded prayer before His death fills the void. *"Praise be to you, O Lord, God of our father Israel, from everlasting to everlasting. Yours, O Lord, is the greatness and the power and the glory and the majesty and the splendor, for everything in heaven and earth is yours. Yours, O Lord, is the kingdom; you are exalted as head over all."* (1Chronicles 29:10-11)

Finally, I take time to listen. Occasionally He has a thought or word for me. At other times I simply know His Spirit wishes to refresh my spirit with His peace and joy. That thought is enough for me.

Call on His Name

Now that we have come full circle, we understand that all communication rests in the desire, the need, and the will to call on His name. *"Call to me and I will answer you and tell you great and unsearchable things you do not know."* (Jerermiah 33:3)

As we seek His face, rest in Him, hold to the quiet times, call upon His name, and abide in His word, He **will** tell us great and unsearchable things we do not know. All knowledge, all understanding, all wisdom rests in Him and in Him alone. To forget the past, to deal with today and to escape fear of the future, He must remain our all in all.

In Christ, God is revealed. By Christ, love is manifested. Through Christ, our life changes and is never the same. We become new creations; the old is gone, the new has come. Because He willingly covered Himself with the stench of our sin and carried it to the cross, His righteousness now rests on us. We are free from sin but free to serve and communicate with Him. Praise God for His goodness!

14. Digging into His Word

When he had finished washing their feet, he put on his clothes and returned to his place. "Do you understand what I have done?" he asked them..."Now that I, your Lord and Teacher, have washed your feet, you also should wash one another's feet. I have set you an example that you should do as I have done for you." John 13:12,14-15

The precious feet of Jesus – covered with dust from traveling, adored by those who loved Him, knelt at by those whom He healed, washed with tears – now took on the role of a servant. No Rabbi Teacher dared humble himself in this manner. Yet this Rabbi changed the rules. Those who followed Him must become servants – His servants. Life thinking must be changed and attitudes altered.

Sacrifices in our Christian walk emerge before us regularly. Among those is the sacrifice of time – time spent with the Master. He awaits our fellowship, He desires our attention, He hears our call – all because of a love beyond all comprehension – a love that gave its all on Calvary.

Refresh yourself with reminders of all the aspects of prayer. Absorb His goodness and remember – *Through Jesus, therefore, let us continually offer to God a sacrifice of praise – the fruit of lips that confess his name.* Hebrews 13:15

Approach the Father - Jeremiah 33:3

Pray in Jesus' name - Hebrews 4:14-16

Desire the Father's will - Hebrews 13:20-21

Crave the Holy Spirit's help - Romans 8:26

Understand His healing - Matthew 11:28-30

Ask - Am I worthy? - Romans 8:1-2

Overcome unbelief - John 15:7-8,16

Be persistent - Luke 18:6-8

Pray for others - Matthew 18:19-20

Claim promises - Psalm 145:13

Be thankful - 2 Corinthians 2:14

Praise - Psalm 138:1-3

Give God the glory - Philippians 2:10-11

Sit at His feet - Luke 10:41-42

Prayer: Jesus, as I approach Your throne of grace, I pray for a vision of prayer. Through Your Spirit, touch my heart with the awesome privilege and potential granted in prayer to those who believe. Burden my heart with a yearning for Your presence and a commitment in communication. May I never cease to ask, seek and knock for Your wisdom and guidance as I journey through this life with You lighting the way. In Your name I pray. Amen

Printed in the United States
1180000001B/169-237